FLOWERS
FALL

FLOWERS FALL

A Commentary on Dōgen's *Genjōkōan*

HAKUUN YASUTANI

Foreword by Taizan Maezumi

Translated by Paul Jaffe

SHAMBHALA
Boston & London
1996

Shambhala Publications, Inc.
Horticultural Hall
300 Massachusetts Avenue
Boston, Massachusetts 02115
www.shambhala.com

Printed in the United States of America

Distributed in the United States by Random House, Inc.,
and in Canada by Random House of Canada Ltd

LIBRARY OF CONGRESS CATALOGING-IN-PUBLICATION DATA

Yasutani, Hakuun, 1885–1973
    Flowers Fall: a commentary on Dōgen's Genjōkōan/Hakuun Yasutani;
    foreword by Taizan Maezumi; translated by Paul Jaffe.—1st ed.
      p.   cm.
    ISBN 1-57062-674-X (alk. paper)
    1. Dōgen, 1200–1253. Shōbō genzō. Genjō kōan. 2. Sōtōshū—Doctrines.
    I. Jaffe, Paul. II. Dōgen, 1200–1253. Shōbō genzō. Genjō kōan.
    English. III. Title.
    BQ9449.D654S53388   1996   96-16433
    294.3'85—dc20   CIP

BVG 01

To My Teachers, Parents, and All Sentient Beings;
and especially to Taizan Maezumi Roshi,
who devoted the greater part of his life
to spreading the Dharma in the West;
and to Tulku Urgyen Rinpoche,
whose teachings have been
of inestimable value.
Their passing is
a great loss.

CONTENTS

Foreword by Taizan Maezumi *ix*

Acknowledgments *xiii*

Translator's Introduction *xvii*

Flowers Fall *1*

Text of the *Shōbōgenzō Genjōkōan* *101*

Notes *109*

Bibliography *129*

FOREWORD

❧ ❧

THE Japanese version of Yasutani Roshi's *Shōbō-genzō Genjōkōan* commentaries was published in the spring of 1967 by Shunjū Publishing Company. Soon after its publication, Yasutani Roshi sent a copy to me with a message written with red ink and in his own hand. It read, "I'm sending this to you to translate into English whenever you feel like it in the future. You may eliminate the unnecessary parts for the English-speaking reader." As a matter of fact, in preparing to write this foreword, I browsed through his various writings and even after all this time, I found myself with renewed feelings of amazement at how energetically he wrote during the last fifteen years of his life, after he turned seventy. Now twenty-six years after his request, this translation by Paul Jaffe is being published. Paul spent over ten years translating this text. I am quite pleased with his effort and appreciate his command of the Japanese language, which enables him to convey clearly Yasutani Roshi's intent and style of expression.

Since Paul has written rather extensively in the translator's introduction about Yasutani Roshi's life and his style of teaching, I should like to mention his contributions to both the followers of Zen and to Buddhist practice in a broader sense. After 1965, Yasutani Roshi wrote two volumes each on the *Mumonkan* and *Shōyōroku*, giving different styles of commentaries. One of the commentaries is direct, short, and sharp—in the style of dialogues in koan form. The other style is a longer commentary that is easier for the general reader to understand. A close dharma friend, who teaches at universities in Japan and also leads a zendo, has told me that he holds these commentaries in very high regard. Given the different styles, he feels that it is remarkable how Yasutani Roshi retained the subtle implications of the original.

Yasutani Roshi also wrote commentaries on *Denkōroku,* the *Blue Cliff Record,* the Five Ranks, the Three Treasures, the Three Pure Precepts, and the Ten Grave Precepts. These were all written over a ten-year period. After this, he began writing commentaries on the *Shōbōgenzō.* His commentary on *Genjō-kōan* was published in 1967, and those on *Sansuikyō* (Mountain and Rivers Sutra) and *Uji* (Being Time) in 1968. This was followed by his commentaries on *Bendōwa* (Endeavor of the Way) in 1970; *Keisei Sanshiki* (Sound of the Valley Streams and Color of the Mountains), *Raihai Tokuzui* (Bowing and Gaining the Marrow), and *Busshō* (Buddha Nature) in 1972.

I still remember vividly Yasutani Roshi's visit to the Zen Center of Los Angeles in 1967, the year that his *Genjōkōan* commentary was published in Japan. That was also the year that I started the Zen Center of Los Angeles. I studied with him from 1962, during his first visit to the United States, to

1968, the year of his last visit. After that, I visited him in Japan in order to finish my formal koan study with him, which I completed on the middle day of the autumn equinox, September 21, 1969.

Owing to my study with Yasutani Roshi, I decided to finish koan study with Kōryū Roshi, whose lineage was through Master Inzan in Hakuin Zenji's line. If it were not for both of them, my benevolent teachers, and the koan study I did with them, I could not have done my part in sharing the dharma with the sangha members of the Zen Center of Los Angeles, regardless of whether or not the way I practiced was traditionally adequate or inadequate as far as the Soto tenets are concerned.

As you read Yasutani Roshi's commentary of the *Genjō-kōan,* you will notice certain critical comments on how *shikan-taza* and koans are practiced. As a matter of fact, this is what Dōgen Zenji himself teaches—the way of practice as the realization of koan, which is the title of this fascicle. As Yasutani Roshi mentions, *genjōkōan* means "each segment of our life, all phenomena in the world, are nothing but the *genjōkōan.*" He interprets for us how to appreciate one's life as the manifestation of koan.

Many commentaries have been written on *Shōbōgenzō,* especially on the *Genjōkōan* fascicle. In 1263, ten years after Dōgen Zenji's death, Senne, who is considered by some scholars to be one of Dōgen's formal successors, finished his own *Genjōkōan* commentary. Senne's commentary is based on the notes he took on Dōgen Zenji's actual talks and also on the notes taken by Jakko, his dharma brother. Forty-five years later in 1308, Senne's successor Kyōgō completed a commentary on *Genjōkōan* based on Senne's talks. In Kyōgō's commentary, he states that although each of the seventy-five fascicles of *Shōbōgenzō* have different titles, they are all *genjōkōan*. According to Kyōgō, "Even though each fascicle discusses different aspects, there is one underlying principle of nonduality or wholeness—i.e., no subject/object and no this/that. Only the principle of undividedness or wholeness is emphasized. Throughout *Shōbōgenzō*—from *Genjōkōan,* the first fascicle, up through *Shukke* (Home Departure), the last or seventy-fifth fascicle—the same underlying principle of oneness is expressed."

Among these old writings, I should also like to mention another unique commentary by Giun Zenji, the fifth abbot of Eiheiji. Giun Zenji wrote appreciatory verses and capping phrases for sixty of the seventy-five fascicles. For *Genjōkōan,* Giun Zenji's capping phrase is *"Kore nan zo"* or "What is this." Throughout Yasutani Roshi's commentary, you will notice how he repeatedly emphasizes the importance of "What is this."

As the epilogue to the original *Shōbōgenzō Genjōkōan* indicates, *Genjōkōan* was written and given to Yō Kōshū, a lay person living in the northern part of Kyūshū. His understanding of Zen must have been splendid in order for Dōgen Zenji to have written such an essay for him. In 1252, just a year before he died, Dōgen Zenji placed *Genjōkōan* as the first fascicle of his seventy-five-fascicle version of *Shōbōgenzō.* From this we can see just how deeply he valued *Genjōkōan.*

—TAIZAN MAEZUMI ROSHI

ACKNOWLEDGMENTS

SINCE the work on this book has been done inter-
mittently over a long number of years, I am indebted to a great number of people, some of
whom I have probably forgotten to mention. I beg
their indulgence for the frailties of human memory.

First and foremost I am indebted to Maezumi Taizan
Roshi. Not only did he introduce me to this book and generously answer many questions about its contents, but he also
guided me in my practice so that I could clarify experientially
at least a few basic points, thus avoiding numerous mistakes
I would probably have made otherwise. Other teachers and
members at the Zen Center of Los Angeles expressed interest
and support, and created a living context for pursuing the
meaning of the text.

Robert Aitken Roshi generously took time to discuss Yasutani Roshi and passages of the *Genjōkōan* with me, and encouraged me to bring the work to completion. Members of his

Diamond Sangha, David Steinkraus and T. Matthew Ciolek, transferred typescript and manuscript onto computer.

In the early days of my work, I benefited from reading sections of the text under the tutelage of Professors Zenryu Shirakawa and Robert Zeuschner. Dr. Peter Gregory has taken time to look over the translation and introduction at various stages of the work, and made numerous valuable suggestions. Dr. John Maraldo gave me the benefit of his thoughtful reflections on the text. Dr. Francis Cook looked at the *Shōbōgenzō* with me over sherry on several occasions. Rick Fields lent me his unpublished manuscript, *Zen in America*.

I am indebted to The Institute for the Study of Buddhist Culture and to Professor Asaeda Zensho of Ryukoku University for an appointment as a Visiting Researcher, thereby making available to me both a visa and an office for a year in 1984–1985. Many of my colleagues at Ryukoku University have been very helpful in resolving linguistic problems and locating references. I am particularly grateful to Mr. Esho Shimazu and Professors Tom Wright, Hiromi Yoshimura, and Hisao Inagaki. Professor Inagaki's *A Glossary of Zen Terms* has been very useful in the last stages of my translation. Dr. Robert Rhodes of Otani University gave me valuable comments on a draft of the introduction. Bonnie Myotai Teace kindly took time to assist me with my final edit of the introduction, and along with John Daido Loori, sensei, engaged me in a thoughtful discussion on the implications of certain terminology.

The First Zen Institute of America did me a great service by sending me one of their last three copies of *Zen Dust*. It has been well used over the years.

Among the growing community of Dōgen translators there has been an ongoing interchange over many years. The pioneering translations of Abe Masao and Norman Waddell have been very useful, as has been the work of Maezumi Roshi, Aitken Roshi, Tanahashi Kazuaki, Francis Cook, Carl Bielefeldt, Okumura Shōhaku and Tom Wright.

I would like to thank the Shunjūsha Publishing Company and Reverend Yasutani Ryoju for kindly granting me permission to publish an English translation of original text. Thanks are due to David O'Neal, Peter Turner, Jonathan Green, and the staff of Shambhala Publications for their efforts in seeing this book into print.

I would also like to thank my parents, Bernard and Edith Jaffe, who have always offered me loving encouragement in my studies.

While a great many people have thus contributed to this work, any shortcomings and inaccuracies are solely my responsibility.

TRANSLATOR'S
INTRODUCTION

☙ ☙

I T seems fitting that the first full-length commentary on
Zen master Dōgen's *Shōbōgenzō Genjōkōan* to be made
available to a Western audience is that of the Zen master
Hakuun Yasutani, one of the most influential figures in
the establishment of Zen in the West. Thus, in a context
which bespeaks the transmission of Zen from China to Japan
to America, and more broadly from the East to the West, we
have a text which focuses on what is quintessential to this
transmission wherever it may take place.

Among Dōgen's many writings, *Genjōkōan* is the one he
chose to place at the beginning of his magnum opus, the *Shōbōgenzō*. In terse and poetic form it addresses a host of important
issues for the understanding of Buddhism, and is often referred to as the key to or outline of the *Shōbōgenzō* (Treasury
of the True Dharma Eye). This work, originally written as a

letter to a lay disciple, remains essentially unchanged in a revised version written almost twenty years later near the end of Dōgen's life, indicating it to contain the consistent core of his teaching.

It is been over twenty years now since the *Genjōkōan* first appeared in English, and several excellent translations exist in English and other Western languages. The text is used as a guide in Zen communities, studied by scholars, and speculated upon by the increasing number of philosophers who are attempting to span cultural boundaries. Yet, in spite of (or perhaps because of) the difficulties of understanding what *Genjōkōan* presents for most readers, those who cannot read Japanese have had to content themselves with a single abbreviated commentary[1] and miscellaneous comments. It is hoped that this book may in some small way add to the understanding and aspiration of those pursuing the dharma.

The Historical Background of Buddhism in Modern Japan

Yasutani Hakuun (1885–1973) was born in the Meiji era (1868–1912), a period when Japan had opened its doors to the outside world for the first time in two and a half centuries. Whatever sectarian lines were already established had become progressively more rigid during the Edo period (1600–1868), during which the Tokugawa government tightly regulated all segments of society, and during which Buddhist institutions were used by the government to help control the populace.

The Edo period came to an end with the Meiji Restoration, nominally restoring the emperor to power. This shift in power also led to a reaction in the form of the *haibutsu kishaku* (abolish Buddhism and renounce Shakyamuni) movement, a politically motivated attempt to suppress Buddhism and establish a form of neo-Shintoism as the state religion. Government suppression and rhetoric also encouraged many citizens to vent their frustration at Buddhist institutions for their complicity with the previous highly repressive government. As a result many temples were destroyed, monks were returned to lay life, and sources of financial support were taken away. At the same time, a sudden influx of information came from outside Japan, and Japanese could travel abroad relatively freely.

Along with the rest of Japan, Buddhism was set upon a search for a renewal of its identity. This especially found expression in two directions: a search for the roots of the tradition, and various varieties of universalism, such as attempts to create a universal, nonsectarian Buddhism. The latter was often suppressed as the state moved in the direction of reasserting the divinity of the emperor and promoting Shinto deities. Again during this time, under great duress, the Buddhist institutions made a great deal of accommodation, in both thought and behavior, to the state.

The established Buddhist sects were, and continue to be, responsible for a great deal of scholarship, which has done much to broaden the horizons of Japanese Buddhism. However, they are still criticized in many quarters as having lost their spiritual vitality. The established institutions tended rather strongly toward the side of maintaining sectarian orthodoxy in the service of protecting tradition, a value deeply etched in the Japanese psyche.

The movement for change, renewal, and adaptation to the religious needs of the populace came primarily from reform movements, many of which were marginal in terms of the major sects, and from the "new religions," which multiplied rapidly during the Meiji period, and except for periods of heavy government suppression, have continued to emerge right up to the present. These new religious movements have in turn acted as a stimulus for change within the established sects. This pattern has been repeated many times in the history of Japanese religion.

When looked at from the perspective of Japanese institutional history, Yasutani may be considered marginal in the sense that he gradually moved more and more out of the mainstream of the Zen establishment. Looking at the overall movement of religion in modern Japan, however, it may be more accurate to view him as a moderate figure, closer to the conservative guardians of tradition than to the new religions, which connected to the old traditions only tenuously or discarded them altogether.

Most of the "innovations" he made have precedent in the Zen tradition. He emphasized the need for reform while looking to the ancient patriarchs for his moorings. With his deep concern for and energetic promotion of lay Zen, he strove to redress an imbalance that has caused deep dissatisfaction with Japanese institutional Buddhism in general. The failure to provide sufficient opportunity for deep religious involvement is in part a carry-over from the Edo period, when government support for temples and the bureaucratic functions of priests caused many of them to become distant from and unresponsive to the needs of the community.

The criticisms Yasutani makes of modern-day Soto Zen may be seen to arise in part from its seeming to have little room for the type of inner searching he went through, which in many ways fit the classical description of the "great doubt," often referred to in koan Zen. Further, much of his criticism is aimed at Nishiari Bokusan (1821–1910), with whom Yasutani had a close relationship in his youth, and who is considered one of the preeminent Soto Zen teachers and *Shōbōgenzō* commentators in the modern period. Yasutani was also one of the major proponents of lay Zen practice, which has had a particularly important impact on the development of Zen in the West. These, among other reasons, make it interesting and instructive to look at the circumstances and events of his life.

A Biographical Sketch of Yasutani Hakuun

There is a miraculous story about Yasutani's birth: His mother had already decided that her next son would be a priest, when she was given a bead off a rosary by a nun who instructed her to swallow it for a safe childbirth. When he was born his left hand was tightly clasped around that same bead. By his own reckoning, "Your life . . . flows out of time much earlier than what begins at your own conception. Your life seeks your parents."[2] "It is as if I jumped right into this situation since while I was still in her womb my mother was contemplating my priesthood." When he studied biology in school this story seemed ridiculous, but later he came to consider it karmically logical. "Now, practicing the Buddha Way more and more, understanding many more channels of the Buddha Way, I realize that it is not so strange but quite natural. My mother wanted me to become a priest, and because I was conceived in that wish and because I too desired the priesthood, the *juzu* [rosary] expressed that karmic relation. There is, indeed, a powerful connecting force between events. We may not understand it scientifically, but spiritually we know it is so." So, in time he came to fully accept this story and treat it as a concrete symbol of "his deep Dharma affinity."[3]

Born into a poor family, he was adopted at the age of five and went to live in a country temple named Fukuju-in near Numazu City in Shizuoka Prefecture. His head was shaved

and he was educated by the abbot, Tsuyama Genpō. His training at this time was very strict and meticulous but also very
loving, and it left a deep impression on him throughout his
life. At the age of eleven he moved to a nearby temple, Dai-
chūji, which like Fukuju-in belonged to the Rinzai sect. After
a fight with an older student, however, he was forced to leave.
When later he was placed in another temple, this time it was
one of the Soto sect, Teishinji, and it was here that he became
a monk of the Soto sect under the priest Yasutani Ryōgi, from
whom he took his name.

At the age of sixteen he went to study under Nishiari Bokusan at Denshinji in Shimada, Shizuoka Prefecture, and
served as his attendant. Nishiari is well known both for having
served as the leader of the Soto sect, and for his *Shōbōgenzō
Keiteki. Keiteki* is a record of his lectures on twenty-nine chapters of the *Shōbōgenzō* and is generally considered an important and authoritative work. Yasutani says of *Keiteki:*

> Beginning with Nishiari Zenji's *Keiteki,* I have closely exam-
> ined the commentaries on the *Shōbōgenzō* of many people
> in modern times, and though it is rude to say it, there are
> an exceedingly large number of places where they have
> failed to grasp its meaning. . . . It goes without saying that
> Nishiari Zenji was a priest of great learning and virtue, but
> even a green priest like me will not affirm his eye of satori.
> . . . The resulting evil of his theoretical Zen became a sig-
> nificant source of later degeneration. . . . So it is my earnest
> wish, in place of Nishiari Zenji, to correct to some degree
> the evil he left, in order to requite his benevolence, and
> that of his disciples, which they extended to me over many
> years.[4]

Further, he tells us that during this period of his life, when he
was sixteen or seventeen, he had two questions. The first was

why neither Nishiari nor his disciples gave clear guidance concerning *kenshō* when it was obvious from the ancient writings that all the ancestors experienced it. There is a parallel here between Yasutani's autobiographical understanding and the account of Dōgen's quest in the traditional biographies. Dōgen is said to have been afflicted by a great doubt about the need for arousing the mind that seeks enlightenment and for undertaking strenuous practice, when the *Mahaparinirvana Sutra* clearly states that "all sentient beings without exception have the buddha-nature." In the case of both Dōgen and Yasutani, the tension of a seeming contradiction between the notion of inherent enlightenment and the need for the practical cultivation of experience spurred them on in their search. It is difficult to guess to what extent the traditional biography of Dōgen formed a paradigm for self-understanding in the mind of Yasutani as a young monk or later as a Zen master. His second question concerned what happens after death. For many years he was unable to resolve his doubts about these questions.

His experience of not being able to receive clear guidance from Nishiari regarding these points was influential in his eventually writing this commentary. "The reason why I criticize *Keiteki* with such severity is that many people in modern times take it as their sole guide to the study of the *Shōbōgenzō*, and I grieve the fact that as a result there are many who misunderstand Dōgen Zenji's rightly transmitted Buddha-dharma."[5]

Through his twenties and thirties Yasutani continued his training with several other Buddhist priests, primarily disciples of Nishiari. He also furthered his education, going to a teacher training school and then beginning a ten-year career as an elementary school teacher and principal. At thirty he married and started raising a family, which was to produce five children.

In 1925, at the age of forty, he returned to his vocation as a Buddhist priest. Soon after, he was appointed as a Specially Dispatched Priest for the Propagation of the Soto sect, traveling around giving lectures. "However," he wrote later, "I was altogether a blind fellow, and my mind was not yet at rest. I was at a peak of mental anguish. When I felt I could not endure deceiving myself and others by untrue teaching and irresponsible sermons any longer, my karma opened up and I was able to meet my master Daiun Shitsu, Harada Sōgaku Roshi. The light of a lantern was brought to the dark night, to my profound joy."[6]

Harada Sōgaku (1870–1961) was a Soto priest educated at the Soto sect's Komazawa University, where he later taught Buddhism for twelve years. His sincere searching brought him to study with Toyota Dokutan, one of the leading Zen masters of his day (1841–1919), abbot of Nanzenji, the head temple of the branch of Rinzai Zen known by the same name. When Harada became abbot of Hosshinji after finishing his studies, he transformed it into a rigorous and lively training center, combining elements of the training he received in the Soto and Rinzai lines.

Yasutani sat his first sesshin with Harada in 1925 and two years later at the age of forty-two was recognized as having experienced *kenshō*. Some ten years later he finished his koan study and then, at the age of fifty-eight, he received dharma transmission from Harada on April 8, 1943, the day the Buddha's birth is celebrated in Japan.

In 1954 Yasutani established his organization as an independent school of Zen. The group, Sanbōkyōdan (Fellowship of the Three Treasures), broke with the Soto school in which Yasutani was ordained, asserting a position of direct connection with Dōgen and no longer recognizing the authority of the sect's ecclesiastical leaders.

Yasutani's career as a Zen teacher was devoted and single-minded. He was head of a training hall for monks for a short while at Zuiganji, a monastery in northern Japan, but he gave it up in order to focus on completing his training with Harada so that his life would be deeply established in the dharma.[7] After that, his efforts were directed primarily toward the training of lay practitioners. His years leading a family life and working as an educator no doubt both influenced him in this direction and prepared him for the task. During the next thirty years he held over three hundred sesshins, led numerous regular zazen meetings, and lectured widely. In addition, he left almost one hundred volumes of writings.

Influence on Zen in the West

Yasutani Roshi first traveled to the United States in 1962 when he was already in his late seventies, at the instigation of some of his American students. He held sesshins in over half a dozen cities, and due to an enthusiastic response he made six more visits through 1969, also teaching in England, France, and Germany. He has exerted a profound influence on the budding Western Zen tradition through direct contact with many students and through his relationships with several of the leading Zen teachers in America. Yasutani has also become widely known and has indirectly influenced many people through the book *The Three Pillars of Zen,* compiled by Philip Kapleau. It contains a short biographical section on Yasutani Roshi and also his "Introductory Lectures on Zen Training," "Commentary on the Koan *Mu,*" and the somewhat unorthodox printing of his *dokusan* interviews with Western students.

Kapleau, who founded the Rochester Zen Center in 1966, was the first Westerner to study with Yasutani. This was in 1956, after Kapleau had studied for three years at Hosshinji under the guidance of Harada Sōgaku. After some twenty sesshins with Yasutani, the master confirmed Kapleau's *kenshō* experience, which is one of the cases set down in *The Three Pillars of Zen*. It was Kapleau who first suggested to Yasutani Roshi that he visit America.

Another of Yasutani's early American students was Robert Aitken, who first sat with him in 1957. Aitken, along with Kapleau, was instrumental in arranging Yasutani's original journey to the United States and, on that and subsequent trips, hosted him for sesshins at Koko-an, his small Zen center in Honolulu, and in 1969 at the newly established Maui Zendo. Aitken says of Yasutani, his only teacher during this period, "He devoted himself fully to us. We felt from him the importance of intensive study, of dedication, and also something of lightness." Aitken further characterizes him as "like a feather but still full of passion," and having "a ready laugh."[8] Aitken studied further with Yasutani Roshi and his successor Yamada Kōun and received transmission from Yamada in 1974.

Shimano Eido first met Yasutani in 1962 when he was a young monk who had spent about two years in Hawaii.[9] His own teacher Nakagawa Sōen took him to meet Yasutani one day. Sōen was planning a trip to the United States and invited Yasutani to join him, which he agreed to do. Then he invited Eido to go along also. Shortly before the trip Sōen canceled his plans due to the illness of his mother. Eido was left to accompany Yasutani as his attendant and translator. The following year Eido again accompanied Yasutani to America and they continued on around the world together. At Sōen's request Yasutani guided Eido in his koan study. Later, Eido wrote, "During his seven times teaching pilgrimage, from the very beginning to the end, I was fortunate enough to serve him as an attendant monk and as an interpreter. I received great teaching from him in many ways. . . . He was a brilliant master.[10]

Maezumi Taizan first met Yasutani in Los Angeles where he was serving as a priest in the Soto Zen Mission in Los Angeles. In addition to having been born into, and raised, educated, and trained in the Soto tradition, Maezumi had also done koan study with the Rinzai lay master Ōsaka Kōryū. When Yasutani Roshi came to Los Angeles, Maezumi started to do koan study with him while acting as interpreter and assisting his sesshins in Los Angeles, where Maezumi established the Los Angeles Zendo (later Zen Center of Los Angeles) in 1968. Between Yasutani's several trips to America and Maezumi's trips to Japan to continue his study, a close relationship developed, culminating with Maezumi's dharma succession in 1970.

Yasutani's influence on these four, each of whom has established a major place in Western Zen, was particularly strong. Many others who eventually became Zen teachers in the West also practiced under his tutelage. In addition, a large number of people had their lives deeply affected by their contact with him. The huge impact he was able to have in the West is certainly due at least in part to his intense devotion to practice and realization, along with his willingness to temper tradition with change, a value of great prominence in the modern Western, and especially the American, psyche.

There is no way to measure the impact he had. It certainly cannot be summed up either in Japan or the West by any kind

of institutional accounting, and it may take a long time before
it can be gauged.

Dimensions of Controversy

In a society where the values of harmony and face-saving are
dominant, the openness with which Yasutani expressed sharp
criticism is rare. We have already recognized that he aimed
to establish a counterpoint to some of the trends he saw in
contemporary Japanese Buddhism. To clarify his position, we
can inquire further into the nature and rationale of his criticism. Yasutani was so outspoken because he felt that the Soto
sect, in which he was ordained and trained, emphasized the
intrinsic or original aspect of enlightenment—that everything,
as it is, is buddha-nature—to the exclusion of the experiential
aspect of actually awakening to this original enlightenment.
Yamada Kōun, his chief dharma successor, has written, "His
main purpose was to propagate the indispensable place of *kenshō*, realization of the Way, in Zen."[11] On the other hand he
criticized the tendency in the Rinzai sect to become attached
to levels and rankings, and the efficacy of koans without adequate regard to the realization of emptiness to which many of
the koans point. He viewed Rinzai and Soto as two sides
of the same coin, and warned against attachment to form at
the expense of the proper understanding and true experience
of Zen.

Though historically it has not necessarily been the case,
generally speaking, a rather wide gulf separates the two main
branches of modern-day Japanese Zen. It is somewhat rare to
find Zen masters who, like Yasutani and his teacher Harada,
have been trained deeply in both Soto and Rinzai traditions.
Yasutani expresses his feeling that there is need for correction

or reform of both sects. In particular, on the Soto side he takes to task those who inappropriately denigrate the idea of enlightenment and suggests that it plays a big role in causing the Soto sect to decay into lifeless intellectualization. "In the end it leads to the mistaken idea that the Buddha-dharma of Eihei Dōgen and the Buddha-dharma of Rinzai are different" (see chapter 8). While acknowledging differences of teaching method in the Soto and Rinzai schools, he emphasizes the essential unity of Zen, quoting Dōgen's statement from *Bendōwa*, "Though there are five houses [of Zen in China], they are just one buddha-mind-seal."

His especially sharp criticism of the Soto sect seems to reflect a certain bond he felt with it even though he officially established Sanbōkyōdan as an independent organization. His references to Soto are usually made merely using "the sect." Perhaps his feelings are most succinctly summed up with his statement, "I'm afraid Dōgen Zenji's Buddha-dharma will vanish from the sect like clouds and mist" (see chapter 7). In trying to distinguish sharply the teachings of those who have thoroughly penetrated the teachings from those who have not, Yasutani has precedent in Dōgen himself, who frequently indicates examples of both complete and insufficient teachings. Whatever other motivations he may have had, in part at least this is a teaching tool. In *Shōbōgenzō Sansuikyō* (Mountains and Rivers Sutra), Dōgen criticizes those who consider the koans of the old masters to be "illogical" and "beyond understanding," saying they "have never seen a true master and they have no eye of understanding. They are immature, foolish fellows, not even worth discussing."[12]

If Yasutani was controversial for his caustic criticisms, it was not only for that. His training style, which he largely inherited from Harada, included plenty of use of the *kyōsaku,* a stick used to keep meditators awake and to spur them on to deeper concentration, as well as vociferous verbal exhortation and communal intoning of "mu," the heart of the first barrier students must pass through in their koan study. The combined effect of these and the otherwise strict atmosphere is sometimes described as a "pressure cooker," designed to drive students beyond their ordinary dualistic perception. Of course shouting and beating found their way into Zen long ago with the line of Huang-po (Ōbaku) and Lin-chi (Rinzai). It is interesting to note that Dōgen's master, Ju-ching, also practiced such severe disciplinary methods. "When the training monks fell asleep during meditation, he made the rounds striking them with his fist or slipper, shaming them and demanding they wake up."[13] According to the early biographies of Dōgen, it was precisely in this type of situation that one of Ju-ching's exhortations, to "drop away body and mind," triggered Dōgen's great awakening.

If one examines the history of the Zen tradition, the most radical innovation in Yasutani's training style may be his systematic introductory lectures, an innovation attributable to Harada. These attempt to communicate systematically the framework for the course of Zen training that the student is about to undertake, and they seem closely related to his effort to make religious experience available to lay people. The degree to which he spoke about *kenshō* and his public acknowledgment of it in a post–sesshin ceremony may be somewhat atypical. At the same time, whether in phrases like "seeing one's nature and attaining the way," "seeing one's nature and attaining buddhahood," "seeing one's original face," or in some other less direct varieties of language, the emphasis on seeing one's true nature has been central throughout the history of the tradition.

Regarding the criticism of Yasutani for overemphasizing *kenshō,* Robert Aitken says, "Yasutani Roshi's hope was that people could get a start, and with that start they could deepen and clarify it through koan study. I think that, actually, Yasutani Roshi placed less emphasis on *kenshō* than the people who are criticizing him, because the people who are criticizing him are regarding *kenshō* as some sort of be-all and end-all, and he didn't look at it that way at all."[14] Also, what may seem like an overblown ceremonial event to Western eyes, often, in Japan's highly formalistic society, is merely a way of giving expression to naturally arising feelings. The feeling of gratitude is one of the acknowledged hallmarks of deep practice.

It is also sometimes suggested that his use of koans along with *shikantaza,* "just sitting," and other elements of Soto Zen, is somehow aberrant. A look at the history of Zen both in China and Japan shows a great deal of cross-fertilization between different schools of Zen, as well as the merging and emerging of different lines. If in modern-day Japan the character of Soto and Rinzai seem rather thickly walled in by the rhetoric of orthodoxy, it was not always so.

Recent research suggests that in medieval Japan the distinction between the Rinzai and Soto schools was less clear and far less important than the distinction between teaching lineages. One example of the extent of the interaction is a Rinzai master who, still dissatisfied with his attainment, subsequently studied koans under a Soto master. After the master's death, he continued his study under several other masters in the same Soto line. Later he met a Soto teacher who had inherited the line of the Rinzai master, Ikkyū Sōjun. At this point they decided to study with each other, so the Rinzai monk instructed the Soto monk in the Soto teaching and vice versa.[15]

One of the major collections of koans, the *Tsung-jung lu* (J. Shōyōroku, "Book of Equanimity"), compiled by two teachers in the Ts'ao-tung (Sōtō) school in China, was completed in 1223, the same year Dōgen arrived in China. Dōgen himself spent between six and nine years at Kenninji, training under Myōzen. Although within the Tendai school, Myōzen transmitted the Huang-lung branch of Rinzai Zen.[16] In *Bendōwa* we find the passage, "Master Myōzen was a great disciple of Ancestor Eisai, from whom he alone received correct transmission of the unsurpassable buddha-dharma."[17]

Dōgen's training there must have focused centrally on koans, for he seems to have gained a broad familiarity with them and assumed meditation on koans to be the mainstay of Zen practice, as shown by his famous dialogue with the cook from A-yu-wang monastery whom he met immediately upon arriving in China. The gist of what Dōgen asked the cook was, "Why is a venerable old monk like you down here shopping for mushrooms instead of meditating upon koans?" Further, when Dōgen returned from China, he brought with him a collection of three hundred koans that he had compiled, known as the *Shōbōgenzō Sanbyakusoku* (Three Hundred Case Shōbōgenzō).

While there is no doubt that "just sitting," denotes something central to the Buddha way for Dōgen, it does not necessarily imply that he did not use koans for training as well. His writings and talks are full of koans and references to koans. According to *Shōbōgenzō Zuimonki* (Dōgen's talks to his monastic community as recorded by Koun Ejō, his chief successor), the master appointed Ejō as the first head monk of Kōshōji, and instructed him to give a talk on the koan "Tung-shan's Three Pounds of Flax."[18] This took place more than nine years after Dōgen's return from China, so it certainly cannot be looked at as a vestige of his earlier training. In fact Dōgen uses the term "just sitting," or close variants, very rarely in his writings. When he uses it to make a contrast, it is not with koan Zen, but with other practices: "Without engaging in incense offering, bowing, chanting Buddha's name, repentance, or reading scriptures, you should wholeheartedly just sit, and thus drop away body and mind."[19] When he frequently criticizes certain proponents of koan Zen, he is criticizing their understanding. Koan Zen itself does not seem to come in for criticism anywhere in his writings. There is nothing that indicates that for Dōgen the principle of just sitting and the use of koans were mutually exclusive, although he certainly distinguished between authentic and incorrect understanding of koans.[20]

Shikantaza is sometimes characterized as sitting in zazen without striving or seeking, and with nothing to be attained and nothing to be realized. The implied characterization, or perhaps caricaturization, of koan zen is that it is a dualistic practice. However, the significance of a koan cannot be truly grasped without taking the "backward step" out of dualistic thinking.[21] In contrast to the criticisms of Nishiari that koan Zen makes zazen secondary, Yasutani says, "This makes it clear that Nishiari Zenji did not know the proper use of koan Zen."[22] Further, he says of koans, "They are something that should be done with exactly the same feeling as a person who has been just sitting *(shikantaza)* for ten, twenty, thirty years" (see chapter 13).

It is possible that the rhetoric of Rinzai as purely koan Zen, and of Soto as the Zen of purely just sitting, may be somewhat of an aberration when viewed historically. This area needs more study to be understood clearly.

If we look at the great Rinzai reformer Hakuin, we can

see him quoting *Genjōkōan,* and making reference to Dōgen's "dropping away body and mind; body and mind dropped away," within a commentary on Tung-shan's Five Ranks, a teaching from the founders of the Soto school that he incorporated into his koan system.[23]

All of this is not to suggest that Yasutani's style is or is not correct, true, or orthodox, but rather that the tradition has undergone many changes, and has seen many styles depending on the perception and personality of the teacher and the social conditions of the time and place. Assertions of orthodoxy emerge from a particular historical context and should be examined from a broad perspective. In themselves they should not be the basis on which we select teachers or try to establish the form of the dharma as it evolves in the West.

This application of rational examination to claims of orthodoxy is a different issue from the question of following the dictates of a teacher to whom one feels committed or karmically linked. In a tradition where authority by definition lies with the teacher, and where trust is a critical factor in going through the difficulties of actual training, evolving a dynamic and lasting tradition out of the tension between these two approaches of rational examination and devoted trust will require the best faculties of both student and teacher.

The Commentary

The *Genjōkōan* is profound and the commentary goes into considerable depth and subtlety. It may be helpful to the reader to identify some of the central themes of the commentary.

In seeking to explicate a balanced understanding of the text, the commentary utilizes two sets of dialectics. The first is movement back and forth between the intrinsic side of inherent (or original) enlightenment and the experiential side of practice and realization. The second dialectic, which in some ways can be seen as overlapping the first, is that of the absolute and the relative. He clarifies these two sides as a basic framework of his commentary right from the start. Taking up the title *Shōbōgenzō* ("Treasury of the True Dharma Eye"), for instance, he discusses the true (or absolute) eye *(shōgen)* and the dharma (or relative) eye *(hōgen)*. He repeatedly stresses, from the intrinsic side, their essential identity, and, from the experiential side, the need for their thorough integration. *Genjōkōan* is treated in a similar manner.

The commentary also uses Dōgen's poetic composition to clarify the different levels of Zen practice, the ways reality can be seen as we progressively deepen our insight and integrate our understanding into our lives. In doing this, he reflects these various ways of seeing in the mirror of other classical Zen teachings, such as the Five Ranks, or Lin-chi's Four Phrases on the Person and the Environment.

Yasutani's extraordinarily deep and broad-ranging knowledge of both Soto and Rinzai literature creates an opportunity for the reader to familiarize himself with key sayings, figures, and writings in the Zen tradition. Toward that end, the translator has as much as possible tried to identify the extensive quotations in the text and to briefly place the figures in historical context. A full treatment would take volumes, but within the limitations of space available, an attempt has been made to direct readers to English language sources where they might find additional information.

Another important characteristic of commentary is its balance of critical (in the sense of rationally analytical) and devotional thought. Since Yasutani was already eighty-two years old when it was first published, he brings virtually a lifetime of study and sincere practice, as well as deep wisdom ripened through decades of teaching, to the jewel that is the *Genjō-kōan*. The depth and subtlety of many sections invite repeated reading to more clearly comprehend the message. The author illuminates the spirit of each passage in a way that seeks to open up our understanding and to encourage us in our faith, practice, and realization. A close reading of this commentary reveals that Yasutani's criticisms are aimed at preserving and restoring the integral balance of these elements in the broad embrace of the Buddha way. It is in this spirit that this translation makes available a small piece of the legacy of Yasutani Hakuun, the Zen master, and of Yasutani Hakuun, the person.

FLOWERS
FALL

What Is Shōbōgenzō?

Shōbōgenzō, or "the treasury of the true dharma eye," is the Buddha way. Shakyamuni Buddha's words to the assembly on Vulture Peak are famous: "I have a subtle teaching of the treasury of the true dharma eye, the wondrous mind of nirvana, the true form of no form. It does not rely on words and is transmitted outside the scriptures. I give it to Mahakashyapa." This also appears in the *Wu-men-kuan.*[1] And so the rightly transmitted Buddha-dharma is called "the treasury of the true dharma eye."

"True dharma" *(shōbō)* is not a relative thing opposed to "false dharma." It's on a different level from the childish words used by some sectarian groups when, like kids squabbling, they establish true and false for their own purposes and say things like, "Our way is the only true dharma and the others are all false dharmas." The whole universe is just this true dharma without a speck of "me." How could this become something to fight about?

Here for the sake of beginners I'll separate the two words *true* and *dharma* and explain them in a manner that is easy to understand. *True* is the world of absolute equality. *Dharma* is the world of absolute differences. Please appreciate the effect of this word *absolute.* It's not simply speaking more emphatically. Absolute means the whole universe is nothing but equality, the whole universe is nothing but differentiation. Therefore, equality and difference are always of the same value. Or rather than "of the same value," they are the same thing. We can't even call them two faces of the same thing. When one says "equality," equality completely swallows up differences (it's not rejecting differences), and differences have no place to show their face. That's what is called absolute equality. Likewise, when one says "difference," differences completely swallow up equality (they're not ignoring equality), and equality has no place to show its face. This is what's called absolute difference. Thus, although the language is the same, the words *equality* and *differences* as they are used in the Buddha-dharma have a completely different meaning from the way they are ordinarily used.

To exhaust the essentials of the Buddha-dharma in a phrase, it's "Buddha-nature/equality, cause-and-effect/differences." To say it more simply it's "emptiness, causes and conditions." "Emptiness" is equality; "causes and conditions" are differences. In the Buddha-dharma the word *equality* means emptiness. In the Buddha-dharma the word *difference* means form, that which has characteristics. In the Soto sect these are called, respectively, the absolute position and the relative position.[2] The absolute position is like an iron bull not having skin or bones. The relative position is like a mud bull having a head and horns. The absolute position is like having a bull made of iron and considering it as being all iron. There are no differences such as skin or bones. The relative position is like having a bull made of mud and regarding it as a bull. When you say it is a bull, it has horns and a head. It comes to be like that because you divide it up again, but if you say it all at once it's just an iron bull, it's just a mud bull.

If we reduce the two words *true dharma* to the level of conceptual thought and explain them, "true dharma" means "emptiness (true), causes and conditions (dharma)." One can also say, as in the *Heart Sutra,* "form (dharma) is emptiness (true)," or "emptiness (true) is form (dharma)." However, thoughts are dead things, they are concepts, not the living reality. Thought can be transmitted by thought, but the living reality cannot be transmitted by thought. So it can't be written in words either. It doesn't rely on words. It's transmitted outside the scriptures. To transmit the living reality there is no other way than for a person who has that actual experience to transmit it to another person who has the same actual experience, without speaking or explaining, by a mind-to-mind transmission[3] in which they come to a mutual total comprehension.

The ninety-five volumes of Japanese dharma words entitled *Shōbōgenzō* are the crystallization of Dōgen Zenji's actual experience of the Buddha way. Therefore, in terms of the Buddha way, to talk about researching the *Shōbōgenzō* conceptually is idiotic. Only upon actually experiencing the true dharma and attaining great enlightenment does one get the flavor of the *Shōbōgenzō* and is then somehow let others taste it a little bit too. Nevertheless those so-called *Shōbōgenzō* scholars since the Meiji period haven't attained this sudden great enlightenment and moreover they ignore, deny, attack, and denounce the enlightened path of seeing one's true nature. Since they give lectures on the *Shōbōgenzō* in that way, a lot of it is just chatter. The important focus becomes completely obscured, and they miss the point. Based on those commentaries people today research the *Shōbōgenzō* conceptually. As a result each person offers his own interpretation, and for this reason again there are many that completely miss the point. For philosophy it may be all right to miss the point, but as for the Buddha way, it's meaningless. In the end they are conceptual amusements and not guideposts for practicing the Buddha way, for experiencing great enlightenment, or for daily life.

In Fuyō Rōran's eighteenth-century commentary on the *Shōbōgenzō, Naippō,*[4] the following words appear: "It is my wish that you plumb the depths of your original self and that you know this treasury of the true dharma eye that you yourself possess." This is telling us to attain great enlightenment and fully open the treasury of the true dharma eye, which each of us has always had. These words are truly a piercing reproach to those who research the *Shōbōgenzō* conceptually. Without a clear eye that sees your own nature and realizes the way, even if you look at the *Shōbōgenzō* you won't be able to grasp its spirit; to say nothing of what a harmful and lifeless thing it is that those who don't have this eye give lectures and write commentaries. Naturally, those who have had only a glimpse of their true nature can hardly appreciate the deep spirit of the *Shōbōgenzō* at all. Only after doing ten or twenty years of grueling practice, in other words, going to *dokusan,* the private interview with the Zen master, and doing strenuous zazen, can we for the first time gradually start to get the flavor of the *Shōbōgenzō*. By practicing as a life-and-death matter, Dōgen Zenji clarified his eye to the point where he could declare, "The great matter of a lifetime search ends here."[5] Since it is a work that, from this wonderful realm, points out the way with each word and phrase, naturally that spirit can't be appreciated by blind children who have neither practice nor realization.

Therefore it's no good to read the *Shōbōgenzō* carelessly. If you are going to read it, you should read it steadily, starting with those chapters that seem easier to understand and gradually progressing to those that seem more difficult. You should read it respectfully, reverently believing that each and every chapter is a great dharma treasure of absolute value, the treasury of the true dharma eye. Even if your eye of the way is not yet clear, it is truly a fine thing if, with a sincere faith in the three treasures and a humble attitude, you just sit and then tranquilly read the text of the *Shōbōgenzō*. But it is extremely foolish to try to discover the spirit of the *Shōbōgenzō* by relying on interpretive commentaries and beginning with the chapters that are difficult to understand. For someone penetrating directly into the *Shōbōgenzō*, these commentaries of mine are also long and useless. So then, regarding the *Shōbōgenzō* itself, it's good enough if you get the flavor of what you can, leaving alone those parts you can't understand. Continuing to exert yourself in the practice of zazen, as your own eye gradually becomes clearer, you will also come to understand more and more. By agreeing with those commentaries which are full of mistakes, and thereupon fancying that you have understood, you fall into an absurdly wrong understanding.

It is said that the *Shōbōgenzō* is something one should read with the whole body. But before being able to read with the whole body, first one must see with the eye of the enlightened way. Opening the eye of the enlightened way means opening the true dharma eye. Now if we break this true dharma eye into two, it comes to be the true eye (also called wisdom eye) and the dharma eye. Opening the true eye is opening the eye of absolute equality. Realizing that there is not a single dharma to be seen in the whole universe, the unenlightened eye is completely destroyed. The world of emptiness has been seen. That "mountains are not mountains and rivers are not rivers"[6] has truly been seen. This is called the wisdom of equality of Manjushri Bodhisattva, or fundamental wisdom.[7] Although there is a difference of depth depending on the person, even with a first glimpse of your true nature, it's the opening of the eye of equality.

Next, opening the dharma eye means opening the eye of absolute differences. It's leaping from "not a single thing"[8] into the realm of the inexhaustible treasury. It's coming to the point where the workings of interdependent existence are seen in clear detail. This is called the wisdom of subtle observation of Samantabhadra, or the subsequently attained wisdom. Regarding the true eye and the dharma eye, we say "one eye is both eyes," and "both eyes are one eye." That's the true dharma eye. In other words it's the eye of the Buddha, the eye of Shakyamuni.

If this buddha eye is clarified you can become a person who is never lacking for all eternity. "The treasure house naturally opens and one receives and uses it freely."[9] That's the treasury of the true dharma eye. In other words each person is a treasure house originally filled with the supreme, ultimate treasure. Not only will the jewel in this treasure house be neither exhausted nor worn out for all eternity, but it is a jewel of wonderful nature and capacity such that the more you use it, the more its brightness increases, the more its capacity increases, the more its functioning increases. How about it? Once you realize that you possess such a treasure, won't each one of you try opening up your treasure house? The key to open wide that treasure house is the ninety-five chapters of *Shōbōgenzō;* it is the one chapter entitled *Genjōkōan;* and within it each word and each phrase is the whole of it. Therefore we can't neglect even one word or phrase.

What Is Genjōkōan?

Next, concerning the word *genjōkōan, genjō* is phenomena. It's the whole universe. It's all mental and physical phenomena. However, it is mental phenomena that ought to be emphasized. But most of the so-called *Shōbōgenzō* scholars put the emphasis on physical phenomena, and moreover, thinking that's an explanation of the whole universe, they forget about what is most important—themselves. Because we repeatedly see and hear this mistake, which is the same one made by Western philosophers, I'm making a special point of mentioning it.

Kōan is derived from the word *official document,* and is used to mean the unerring absolute authority of the Buddha-dharma. So then, *genjōkōan* means that the subjective realm and the objective realm, the self and all things in the universe, are nothing but the true Buddha-dharma itself. However, this is only an explanation of the word. Pay careful attention to the fact that it is not the living *genjōkōan* itself.

So now, what is it that is called the true Buddha-dharma? If in trying to understand it, one calls it the truth, that doesn't completely miss the mark. But this word *truth* is a word that expresses the supreme ideal in Western thought. It's not appropriate to use it as a substitute for the word *Buddha-dharma,* which expresses the original self that pervades the whole universe. In the Buddha-dharma, since ancient times reality has been expressed using the words *true suchness.* So then, the word *way* is more appropriate for expressing the Buddha-dharma, but *way* has many meanings and it's not clear which "way" this is. So in order to distinguish it from the various little "ways," the term *great way* is used. But, since *great way* is a term that was originally used in the teachings of Lao-tzu and Confucius, with this term the Buddha way becomes confused with those ways.

Of course the way of the Buddha and the ways of Lao-tzu and Confucius may have some common aspects, but they can't be said to be exactly the same. They each have their own characteristic contents. In the end, other than saying "the Buddha-dharma," "the Buddha way," or "the supreme way," there are no appropriate words for expressing the way of the

Buddha. Since this is the case, if we paraphrase the word *gen-jōkōan* in ordinary language, it becomes: "The entire phenom-enal world is the living Buddha way."

Although we say "the phenomenal world," it is not limited to the phenomenal world that can be depicted in the human mind. To put it in Buddhist technical language, it means all "direct and indirect karmic circumstances in the ten worlds."[10] To say it in a way that is easier to understand: From the pits of hell at the bottom to the summit of the Buddha realm at the top, all existence, all phenomena, are nothing but the Bud-dha way itself. Yet what is this "Buddha way itself"? Until we clarify what that is, we won't understand its true meaning. It is this one volume entitled *Genjōkōan* that clearly points this out. In other words this single volume is one that painstakingly points out to his disciples the treasury of the true dharma eye, the realization of himself, which Dōgen experienced in thor-oughgoing great enlightenment.

Once again, let's express the substance of the title *Genjō-kōan* in rather concrete terms. *Genjōkōan* means what is mani-fest *(genjō)* is itself absolute reality *(kōan)*. It means all phe-nomena are the supreme way. The supreme way is the original self. People hearing this for the first time are surprised. They can't believe their own ears or eyes. There is no point vacantly gazing off into the distance looking for the supreme way. Isn't it taught in Dōgen Zenji's *Guidelines for Studying the Way* that "the Buddha way is right beneath one's feet"? Or rather, not so much what's under the feet as the feet themselves. The feet are the Buddha way. The hands are the Buddha way. One's whole body and mind are the Buddha way. One's whole life is the Buddha way. Huang-lung indicated this, saying, "Both my hand and the Buddha's hand"; "both my foot and an ass's foot."[11] This is also what is meant by Ma-tsu Tao-i's "Mind is buddha," and "no mind, no buddha."[12] It is also what Dōgen Zenji expresses as "To study the Buddha way is to study the self."

Now look. Having gazed out at the phenomenal world and explained that "that is the Buddha way, that is the manifestation of the truth" is not enough. The whole phenomenal world is entirely oneself. Therefore the clouds, the mountains, and the flowers; the sound of a fart and the smell of urine; earthquakes, thunder, and fire are all the original self. Reading sutras and holding services, telling a pack of lies, slander and idle talk, ugliness and cuteness, everything altogether is supreme enlightenment.

Everything is your original self that is perfectly without lack and is completely fulfilled in itself. Don't be surprised. That's *genjōkōan*. It's in the *Lotus Sutra,* isn't it! It says that there were five thousand people who upon hearing the teaching of the One Buddha Vehicle were greatly amazed, quit the dharma assembly, and left.[13] At that time, Shakyamuni Buddha said, "Good riddance." Don't become one of that good-riddance crowd. Don't misread the phrase "only avoid picking and choosing," found in the opening passage of *Verses on Faith in Mind!*[14] Where is there room for picking and choosing? Where is there room for hating and loving, picking up and throwing away? If even just these two feelings of love and hate are excluded from the supreme enlightenment, then the buddhas and ancestors aren't saying even a single word from the standpoint of the original self. Those who make this kind of mistake are a bunch of blind children who fail to grasp the living words of the buddhas and ancestors and turn them into completely dead words. If you think that the discriminating function of picking up and throwing away, picking and choosing, is outside buddha-nature, then Buddha isn't telling us anything either. It was Dōgen Zenji who clearly and expressly perceived the original text of the *Nirvana Sutra* to be saying "the whole existence of all sentient beings is buddha-nature."[15]

If we look in the books of those teachers who, from the last hundred years or so, are called spiritual guides, scholars, or doctors in the modern Soto sect, how many people are there who really understand the phrase "only avoid picking and choosing"? Looking at it solely from the experiential side, almost all of them are avoiding the universe of the original self, which can be expressed as "the perfect way is without difficulty." In other words they are missing the universe of manifest absolute reality *(genjōkōan)*. At the very beginning of the *Genjōkōan* the phrase "there are delusion and enlightenment" comes leaping out as an expression of "when all dharmas are the Buddha-dharma." How could that be if the Buddha-dharma excludes the deluded views and feelings of picking up and throwing away, hating and loving?

Throwing everything into a big catch-all bag by saying, "Well, everything, whatever it may be, is the Buddha-dharma," doesn't amount to anything. You might say that that's absolute value, but if you take the most important thing, which is yourself, out of the picture, what is absolute value? Who judges value? Even if you try to establish philosophical theories, saying, "Those things each have their own reason for being, their own value in being," that only turns out to be another form of conceptual amusement. It's not living the supreme way of the original self. So then, let me figuratively sum up the fact that everything is the supreme way, everything is the true self.

It's as if the whole universe is nothing but the continuous development of the complete, perfect performance of one great living drama, with all the best actors. Further, this great drama is always limited to one time only. There are never any retakes. And then don't forget the fact that, everywhere and always, the self plays the main part. No, it's not even the main part. To say it truly, it's all the actors plus the stage, the scenery, and small props, the theater and the audience; all are parts of the self, or better, each is the whole of the self; it's a perfect one-man show. To say it another way, the original self is the general manager of the universal drama. Master Hsuan-sha expressed this as, "The whole universe in the ten directions is a tiny shining jewel."[16] Master Ch'ang-sha said, "The whole universe in the ten directions is the single eye of a monk."[17] That's what Shakyamuni Buddha proclaimed as, "Above the heavens and below the heavens, I alone am revered." What do you think? Having this kind of actual experience is a little different from saying, "a manifestation of the truth," isn't it? This is the meaning of Chao-chou's asking, " 'The perfect way is not difficult, only avoid picking and choosing'; What is this 'not picking and choosing'?"[18]

Now, please bear in mind that if you don't take hold of that clear realization by means of a thoroughgoing great enlightenment to the fact that everything is yourself, then the true life of the original self will definitely not emerge, and the mind of great compassion, which is unconditioned and undifferentiated, will definitely not emerge. It is nothing more than conceptual amusement to conditionally affirm that all existence and all activity are manifest absolute reality, as today's sect leaders do when they say, "If you see from the Buddha's standpoint of great compassion. . . ." Even if you understand the theory that everything is the self, that doesn't make even one word of it your own. It's like knowing what's inside another person's wallet. Without doing zazen, without seeing your true nature, no matter how correctly you understand and have faith in the words of the *Shōbōgenzō,* it won't become your own. All the more so with false, distorted understanding. When my teacher Daiun Shitsu [Harada Sōgaku Roshi] gave *teishō* on this chapter, he said, "The philosophy of Nishida is 'the discourse on all phenomena being true existence,' but to what extent has that actual fact been seen? The words resemble the *Genjōkōan.*" For anybody who opens up the *Shōbōgenzō* even a little, the fact that philosophy and the Buddha way are as different as the moon and a snapping turtle, that thought and reality are as different as clouds and mud, will begin to become clear. To sum it up, *genjōkōan* means "everything in a person's life is the living Buddha way." Daiun Roshi also said, "In the seventy-five-chapter version of the *Shōbōgenzō,* this chapter comes first.[19] That's because this chapter is the outline of the *Shōbōgenzō.*" From here we'll enter into a point-by-point commentary on the original text.

When all dharmas are the Buddha-dharma, there are delu-   1
sion and enlightenment, practice, birth, death, buddhas,
and sentient beings. When the myriad dharmas all are with-
out self, there is no delusion, no realization, no buddhas,   ⚘ ⚘
no sentient beings, no birth, and no death. Since originally
the Buddha way goes beyond abundance and scarcity, there
are birth and death, delusion and realization, sentient be-
ings and buddhas.

WHEN all dharmas are the Buddha-dharma"
and "when the myriad dharmas all are without self" confront each other. This is just
the one Buddha-dharma expressed in two
ways. On this point, I've tried reading books by various modern writers, but all of them are superfluous and we can hardly
find any place at all where they directly show the spirit of the
original text.

To speak traditionally, "When all dharmas are the Buddha-dharma," is the "gate of setting up differences."[20] It's the
relative position. But it's not the simple relative position that
the unenlightened person sees. It's the relative position that
has the absolute position as its ground. In other words it's the
relative in the midst of the absolute. If we reduce this "relative
in the midst of the absolute" to philosophical language, and
say "it's affirmation with negation as its ground," conceptually
it seems easy to grasp, but that's a delusion.

As for "when the myriad dharmas all are without self,"

it's the "gate of sweeping away differences." It's the absolute position. The absolute position definitely cannot be pictured in the mind of the unenlightened person. This, also, is not the simple absolute position; it's the absolute position with the relative position as its ground. In other words it's the absolute in the midst of the relative. If you express this "absolute in the midst of the relative" conceptually as "negation with affirmation as its ground," it seems to give you the feeling of understanding, but that also, after all, is a delusion.

Now, both of these two are the perfect *genjōkōan* and not relative. But that is only a one-sided view. If you know a one-sided view to be a one-sided view, and take it up and treat it as a one-sided view, that's fine. But, if you were to hold a one-sided view and think and say that it's the whole thing, then you would be completely mistaken. Daiun Roshi always said this, and it's an important awareness for people who read Buddhist scriptures.

Nishiari Bokusan Zenji[21] takes great pride in driving home the point that these two steps and the third step that follows all have equal value. That's fine if it's a kind of caution to beginners, but it's not a particularly penetrating insight. It's been a general principle of the Buddha-dharma right from the start. However, it's a general principle that stands on the one-sided view of equality of content. When we speak from the side of seeing differences, the fact that the three steps of this passage have their sequential order, with relative importance and depth, has to be grasped on a gut level.

Now, on the one hand there is "all dharmas" and on the other hand "the myriad dharmas," but it's the same thing. When we call all mental and physical phenomena "all dharmas," we also call them "the myriad dharmas." Those are divided up and shown as "when . . . are the Buddha-dharma" and "when . . . are without self." Both are "when." It isn't a position. That "when" is not a hypothetical *when* either. It's the *when* of coming face to face with an actual experience as vivid as blood oozing out of a cut. It's the *when* of having attained great enlightenment and having thoroughly penetrated "all dharmas are the Buddha-dharma." To say it in other words, it's when you've attained great enlightenment and have thoroughly penetrated the fact that all dharmas are the true form, all dharmas are buddha-nature, all dharmas are Vairochana Buddha, all dharmas are *muji,* all dharmas are the original self.[22] The content of that *when* is expressed as "there are delusion and enlightenment, practice, birth, death, buddhas, and sentient beings." "There is practice" is natural. To make it "there are practice and enlightenment" would not be appropriate. What is that "there are"? Of course, it is a word that corresponds to the following "there are no" and is not simply trying to show "there are." In other words, if you awaken and see, it is the fact that delusion and enlightenment, practice, birth, death, buddhas, and sentient beings all are original self, the activity of the original self, and there is nothing else. This kind of understanding is called the relative in the midst of the absolute. In terms of Master Lin-chi's four views, this is equivalent to snatching away the person but not the objective world, and snatching away the objective world, but not the person.[23] This, then, is still the glittering of enlightenment.

In that case, what kind of *when* is "when the myriad dharmas all are without self"? It's when enlightenment has become one step deeper and clearer than before. In other words, it's when the glare of enlightenment has gradually become tempered. With the previous step there was something shining that had a strong stench of the enlightenment in which all dharmas are the Buddha-dharma and all existence is oneself. The sickness of the delusion of having thought from beginningless time that self and others are different, that self and others are in opposition to each other, is just getting completely cured, and now it's like spilling the medicine bottle of the realization that self and others are one body, that everything is oneself.

The *when* of cleaning up after that medicine bottle is "when the myriad dharmas all are without self." It's when "I" and "they" have completely disappeared. It's when the traces of enlightenment have come to an end. It's when you have truly penetrated "originally not one thing." It's "the person and the objective world both snatched away." Therefore it's "no delusion, no enlightenment, no buddhas, no sentient begins, no birth, and no death." Isn't it natural? There's nothing difficult to be scratching your head about. It's when, first having had the great death, there is not even a bit of cloud to obstruct the eye. It's when there is vast darkness. It's the realm that is completely unknown even by all buddhas in the three worlds.[24]

Anyone who whimsically imagines this realm and, being deluded, gives rise to the illusion that he has understood or is reaching the point where he is coming to understand it, is an ignorant fool. Even the words of Confucius, "When you don't know, say you don't know; this is knowledge," when they are carried this far, become an immense thing.[25] Those who have penetrated *muji,* please, also get the source and the point of *muji.*[26] There are differences of depth and clarity, but the thread is the same.

Now, let's compare this with the koan "Feng-hsüeh's Nation," case 61 of the *Blue Cliff Record.*[27] The commentary portion of "Feng-hsüeh's Nation" says: "If you set up a single atom of dust the nation flourishes and the old peasants frown. If you do not set up a single atom of dust the nation perishes and the old peasants sing." The first half is the "gate of setting up differences"; it's "when all dharmas are the Buddha-dharma." The latter half is the "gate of sweeping away differences"; it's "when the myriad dharmas all are without self." However when we say, "It's the gate of setting up," and "It's the gate of clearing away," it becomes two things. It's still half-baked. It's half-dead, half-alive. It doesn't become the truly lived fact. Then, to show the actual living fact, Hsüeh-tou couldn't help but brandish his staff.[28] That's how it is in the koan "Feng-hsüeh's Nation."

In the *Genjōkōan*, the role of Hsüeh-tou holding up his stick is presented by Dōgen Zenji in the following third step. "Since originally it goes beyond abundance and scarcity, the Buddha way has birth and death, delusion and enlightenment, sentient beings and buddhas." "Abundance" is "when all dharmas are the Buddha-dharma." It's the *when* of "there are." "Scarcity" is "when the myriad dharmas all are without self." It's the *when* of "there is no." Speaking from the point of view of meaning, both of these two *whens* are supreme enlightenment *(bodhi)*. They are the original self. Therefore they are of the same value, but looking at it in terms of form, both abundance and scarcity are still incomplete realizations, and moreover, the side of abundance is shallow and the side of scarcity is deep. This is the experiential aspect; in other words, it's speaking from the path of practice.

How is it from the intrinsic standpoint? It goes without saying that going beyond abundance and scarcity is the true reality. Setting up and clearing away are both completely transcended. From the beginning everything is completely transcended. But the two gates of setting up and sweeping away naturally appear out of necessity for the experiential aspect that converts delusion into enlightenment. Therefore, when you return to the original self, you become the originally completely transcendent person you always have been. "There are birth and death, delusion and enlightenment, sentient beings and buddhas." "Neither the person nor the objective world snatched away."

Now the meaning of the "there are" in the first step and of the "there are" in the third step are different. In the first step it is the "there are" of "snatching away the person but not the objective world," and "snatching away the objective world but not the person." In the third step it is the "there are" of "neither the person nor the objective world snatched away." The "there are no" of the second step of "person and objective world both snatched away" has been passed through. These wonderful places should be actually penetrated and actually investigated by each person. I'm being so kind because I'm losing all my virtue. I've already lost a lot, but it can't be helped. Only losing doesn't come to much of a business, does it? But expecting to lose my eyebrows I'll go ahead and pay the price.[29] With this the outline is completed, but up to here it's still explanation. Explanations are dead words. So then Dōgen Zenji expresses live words. I'll say it again. What has been pointed out up to here is an explanation of the *Genjōkōan*. From here he thrusts forth the expression of the living *genjōkōan*.

Yet, though it is like this, simply, flowers fall amid our longing and weeds spring up amid our antipathy.

2

HERE it has to be "yet, though it is like this." With this he makes a complete turn around, and just look at the force of his words, as if he were saying, "Up to here it's been explanation, but from here on I'm going to put forth the real thing."

If one can't distinguish between live words and dead words, can he be called a Zen monk? In other words, the two phrases "flowers fall . . ." and "weeds spring up . . ." are Dōgen Zenji's live words. If you take them up in the *dokusan* room, they make a wonderful koan. If you start to lecture even a little bit you'll be chased out of the *dokusan* room by the master's bell. Simply, flowers fall amid our longing and weeds spring up amid our antipathy! It's just the way it reads. The style of Dōgen Zenji's language is very elevated, so if one's dharma eye is not clear one can't easily grasp what he is saying. If as a result of that you entertain your own personal deluded views, saying things like the flower is a metaphor for enlightenment and the weeds are a metaphor for delusion, it brings you around to the absurd place of saying, "You shouldn't seek after the flower of enlightenment or dislike the weeds of delusion," and it has the negative effect of leading you into advocating an it-doesn't-matter Zen with no practice and no enlightenment.

If we simply paraphrase these expressions of Dōgen Zenji's, it loses its style, but that can't be helped. For the sake of beginners, let's try it. "In last night's storm the beautiful blossoms all fell off. Ah! What a shame. When it rains for two or three days, again the weeds have grown up. Oh, well." Those who know, know that this is the living *genjōkōan*. If you add on a discourse or make an explanation, then the living *genjōkōan* dies right off.

However, looking at several commentaries, they knock these two phrases down to the experiential level as a guide to practitioners and make plausible but specious arguments, saying, "Even though flowers fall, don't regret it. Even though weeds grow, don't hate them. Don't arouse the passions of attraction and repulsion, hating and loving. If only we don't arouse the passions, the falling of flowers and the growing of weeds as they are is manifest absolute reality *(genjōkōan)*" If you look at it in that way, the first thing that happens is that Dōgen Zenji's words die. Even looking at the structure of the sentences you'd think they could understand that it's not something at the level of a pointer for a dull novice monk.

Carrying the self forward to confirm [the existence of] the myriad dharmas is delusion. The myriad dharmas advancing and confirming [the existence of] the self is realization.

3

🌱 🌱

ERE the matter of delusion-and-realization is shown from the standpoint of manifest absolute reality. It's all right to apply this to our practical understanding of how to live in the world, but ultimately the question of application is secondary. It does not have the primacy of the dharma of manifest absolute reality.

The whole of the *Genjōkōan* from here on has the sense of being an elaboration of the first paragraph. It is by no means just a miscellaneous collection of teachings randomly strung together. In this passage Dōgen Zenji clearly and concisely points out the content of that "delusion and realization" in the opening passage, "When all dharmas are the Buddha-dharma, there are delusion and enlightenment. . . ."

Delusion-and-realization is the fundamental problem of the Buddha-dharma. The word *delusion* and the word *realization* as they are commonly used have tremendous differences in depth and scope. We commonly say such things as "climbing the mountain I lost my way," or, "I lost myself over a woman."[30] Then we also say such things as, "I realized that alcohol is no good," or, "I truly realized that up until now I've been fooled by a superstition." But the words *delusion* and *realization* as they are used in the Buddha-dharma have a qualitatively different meaning from that "delusion" and "realization." This also is something I'm explaining for the sake of beginners.

So then, the mind of an unenlightened person is completely deluded. Shakyamuni Buddha calls them sentient beings with upside-down delusions. Daiun Roshi always used to say quite bluntly that philosophical studies are deluded studies, and in fact, that's just calling a spade a spade. If you want to find the authority for it in the Buddhist scriptures, the proof is the precious sayings of the Buddha. Sentient beings are originally buddhas, but there is not one unenlightened person who knows this. Every one of them is just a sentient being with upside-down delusions.

Of the ten realms, excepting only the Buddha realm, the rest of them, from the bottom of hell to the upper reaches beyond the heavenly realms, which are the great bodhisattvas, are all realms of delusion. However, there are naturally tremendous differences within the range of delusion. Therefore even if we arouse the mind that seeks enlightenment, practice the Buddha way diligently, see our true nature, and realize the way, each of these is nothing more than one wave in the sea of delusion. Hence the saying, "To pursue practice in the midst of delusion."[31]

For all sentient beings, realization is completed only after attaining buddhahood. In terms of Tendai's six levels of recognizing identity with the Buddha, this statement corresponds to the level of ultimate identity.[32] That's the meaning of "attaining enlightenment comes before awakening." One becomes enlightened at the time of enlightenment. It's not some strange thing like saying, "We are enlightened before we become enlightened." To say that we are originally enlightened is to speak from the level of the first of the six identities, which is identity in principle. In principle one is originally a buddha,

but as a matter of fact one is seeing the dreams of the unenlightened.

No matter how much one is watching deluded dreams,
one is nothing other than a buddha. All dharmas are the Buddha-dharma. Sentient beings are originally buddhas. That's
how it is when we see with the enlightened eye! Therefore, as
it is, all delusion is manifest absolute reality.

To whatever extent the clouds of delusion break up, to the
same extent the moon of enlightenment increases in brilliance.
Each and all of these various stages are manifest absolute reality. That is identity with the Buddha at the level of partial
truth. To very simply state the essential point of the change
from delusion to enlightenment, it is in the difference between
"carrying the self forward to confirm [the nature of] the myriad dharmas" and "the myriad dharmas advancing and confirming [the nature of] the self." To say it more simply, it's self
and no self. Carrying the self forward to confirm [the nature
of] the myriad dharmas is delusion. Mistakenly discerning a
self, one mistakenly perceives there to be a myriad of things
other than oneself. With this delusion as its basis, no matter
how much cultivation is amassed and no matter what states of
consciousness open up, it's all delusion. "Sentient beings are
deluded; losing themselves, they chase after things."

The myriad dharmas advancing and confirming [the nature of] the self is enlightenment. When the deluded dream
of ego breaks up, you become aware of the fact that all existence is the self. "There is no self in the sage. Because there
is no self, there is nothing which is not self."[33] "Snatch away
the person but not the objective world." It's all objective
world. There is no self. "Simply forgetting all about one's own
body and mind, leaping into the family of the Buddha, one
acts from the side of the buddhas. When you go along in this

way, without either exerting your strength or exhausting your mind, you part from birth and death and attain buddhahood."[34] Parting from birth and death means parting from delusion. Attaining buddhahood means the unfolding of enlightenment.

Those who have great realization about delusion are bud-dhas. Those who are greatly deluded within realization are sentient beings.

4

🌿 🌿

THIS also elaborates upon "there are Buddhas and there are sentient beings," which appears in the opening passage. Here he clearly expresses the meaning of "buddhas" and "sentient beings," and, while implicitly making it ring with an important pointer for the experiential aspect, he shows the universe of the intrinsic aspect and clarifies the fact that everything is manifest absolute reality.

In this section as well, there is no need to make it complicated and difficult. One should just take the words as they are. Enlightened persons are buddhas; those who are deluded are sentient beings. And whether deluded or enlightened, one is manifest absolute reality. One is one's original self, which doesn't increase or decrease by one iota.

Those who have clearly realized that up until now they have been deluded are buddhas. Everyone has always been enlightened or rather, is enlightenment itself, but those who don't know that, and are deluded, are sentient beings. That's us. Therefore just because one becomes enlightened, that doesn't mean anything changes. It's the same as it's always been. But unless one thoroughly realizes that he lacked nothing at all as he was, he absolutely can't become a buddha. And so, one absolutely cannot attain peace and liberation. Since such an important thing is squeezed into a mere two phrases, it's an unusually powerful expression. "Those who have great realization about delusion are buddhas. Those who are greatly deluded within realization are sentient beings."

Further, there are people who attain realization upon real-
ization and people who are deluded within delusion.

5

THIS section goes even further in discussing delusion and realization. In both the first and the second sentences he points to high levels of accomplishment. When realization is mentioned, those who are in the dark about actual practice and enlightenment, thinking it's all the same, mistake a dreamlike glimpse of one's true nature for thoroughgoing great enlightenment. Please understand very clearly that, just as in the saying "even if one ascends Mount Sumeru there are still heavens above,"[35] even though one is enlightened, one further attains enlightenment.

However, in essence there are not several kinds of enlightenment. If it's real enlightenment, whether shallow or deep, it is essentially the same, but in that enlightenment there are tremendous differences in clarity and depth. Therefore, from olden times there is the saying "eighteen great enlightenments and innumerable small enlightenments."[36] Furthermore, understand very well that concerning the maturity or immaturity of their accomplishment, even persons endowed with the same enlightened eye are as different as heaven and earth, or clouds and mud.

"Chao-chou sees through the old woman" is a koan that compares depth of accomplishment and clarity of the eye of Chao-chou with that of an old woman on the road to Mount Tai.[37] "Accomplishment" refers to the degree to which enlightenment itself is assimilated and fused into one with that person's character and life. It's a matter of how much enlightenment becomes one's personality, becomes one's character, becomes one's life. Even though the fact of no-self becomes visible with the enlightened eye, how much has that person *become* no-self? Even though the fact that self and others are one becomes visible with the enlightened eye, it's a question of whether one's daily activity expresses the oneness of self and other. That's what's important.

When one looks at the second clause superficially, it seems as if it is pointing out that in delusion, as well, there are depths beyond depths, and that there are sentient beings who pile up two or three layers of delusion. But looking at it in terms of the sentence structure and the force of words, he is not speaking at such a low level. Rather, we have to see this as something that ties things together by presenting the person who, having plumbed the depths of the great practice, having attained enlightenment upon enlightenment, proceeds further yet.

Fundamentally, such matters as saving sentient beings are the delusions of bodhisattvas. Where are the sentient beings to be saved? From the pits of hell at the bottom, reaching up to the summit of the Buddha realm, there is not even a single deluded sentient being. Every person is breathing through his own nose. Sentient beings are originally buddhas. All are nothing but Tathagatas of pure gold.[38] Is there any saving to be done? At that point one is just a self-improving corpse. One is like a person taking a nap at the very summit of enlightenment. If one has stopped at the intrinsic aspect, what does it amount to?

That's the point, isn't it! It's coming to the realization, or rather the delusion, that the whole universe is oneself. Because one can vividly see that all sentient beings, which are within oneself, are watching deluded dreams and are incessantly suffering, the situation becomes intolerable and one comes to feel that until she saves every one of these pitiful sentient beings, she will not attain true awakening. That is what is called the mind of great compassion that is unconditioned and undifferentiated.

Moved by this mind of great compassion one embarks upon saving sentient beings. However, since the realm of sentient beings is inexhaustible, one's vow also is inexhaustible, and so one immerses oneself eternally in the work of saving sentient beings and just goes on endlessly with the futile, back-breaking task of "carrying snow to fill up a well." That is the practice of the vow of the great bodhisattva who is called "a person who is further deluded within delusion." This is the living Buddha-dharma. This is the spirit of "Each time thinking: 'By what means can I cause sentient beings to attain entrance into the supreme way and speedily attain Buddhahood?' "[39] The same goes for the inclining of the head in deep concern of the wish-fulfilling Avalokiteshvara,[40] and for Kshitigarbha Bodhisattva, who eternally forsakes becoming a buddha.[41]

So then, this means that seen with the enlightened eye of "when all dharmas are the Buddha-dharma," both those who have attained enlightenment upon enlightenment and those who are deluded within delusion are entirely manifest absolute reality, are the Buddha way itself, are the great activity of one's own original nature. That's just as natural as can be.

When buddhas are truly buddhas they do not need to be aware of being buddhas. However, they are actualized buddhas and further actualize buddhahood. 6

HERE again Dōgen Zenji clearly indicates the meaning of buddhas as buddhas. Though we simply say "buddha," from the buddha of identity in principle, which is the buddhahood of one's original nature, to the fully perfected buddha of ultimate identity, "buddha" can be divided into innumerable levels. But, regardless of the level of identity with buddhahood, we can say that whatever one completely assimilates is something that does not rise up to consciousness. It's the same as when food has been completely digested and become blood and there is not any feeling of a full stomach. While you have a full feeling in your stomach, the food you have eaten is still not digested. In the same way as that, when we see our true nature and attain buddhahood and completely absorb that into ourselves, such things as "having become enlightened" and "having become a buddha" do not rise up to consciousness.

Everyone dances for joy, puffed up to the sky with pride, with an attitude of peerlessness because of his piping hot enlightenment. This is still far from having truly become a buddha. When enlightenment is completely digested and the traces are gone, "they do not need to be aware of being buddhas." However, that's the truly actualized buddha. That's further actualizing buddhahood.

In mustering the whole body and mind and seeing forms,
in mustering the whole body and mind and hearing sounds,
they are intimately perceived; but it is not like the reflection
in a mirror, nor like the moon in the water. When one side
is realized the other side is dark.

7

HERE Dōgen Zenji shows the way in which one further actualizes buddhahood. Body and mind are fundamentally one. Regarding them as two is a thought, a delusion. When you are happy, is it your mind that is happy or is it your body that is happy? When you are hungry, is it your body or your mind? If you say, "My stomach has become empty, it must be my body," don't we also say, "I realized how hungry I was?" Then, it must be the mind. Don't be asinine. It's both. Both are one. When mind and body are working separately, neither of them is any good. They are utterly incomplete. The whole idea is extremely frivolous. Be serious. Mind and body are always one.

Here Dōgen Zenji has shown the manner of earnestly practicing the Buddha way. In other words it's completely mustering the whole body and mind. Seeing and hearing, standing and sitting, it's completely mustering the whole body and mind. That's "just," wholeheartedly. It's just walking, just working, just sitting.[42] It's just being in *samadhi* throughout the twenty-four hours of the day. This is the way of practice of our predecessors, the buddhas and ancestors. In modern terms one can call this living fully.

When Master Hsiang-yen was sweeping the garden, he was just working with his whole body and mind completely mustered. Therefore at the single sound of a pebble striking bamboo, he attained great enlightenment.[43] When the priest Ling-yun was on pilgrimage, with his whole body and mind mustered he was just making a pilgrimage and climbing up a mountain road. Therefore, when he glanced at a peach blossom he attained great enlightenment.[44] To intimately perceive is to realize the Way.

Now, between completely mustering the whole body and mind to see forms and to hear sounds, and intimately perceiving (attaining great enlightenment), there is a subtle turning point. These two are not the same. And yet, of course, they are not unrelated. Therein is the subtle experience called "the single sound of enlightenment,"[45] which is spontaneously expressed. Shakyamuni Buddha upon his enlightenment exclaimed, "How wonderful, how wonderful!"[46] Hsiang-yen said, "One striking of the pebble on the bamboo and I have forgotten everything I knew." Ling-yun said, "Having directly arrived at this moment, I have no further doubts."[47] Su Tung-p'o sang out, "The sound of the mountain is this broad, long tongue of the Buddha."[48] Thus, seeing one's true nature and realizing the Way is the basis of the Buddha way. You people of the Soto sect should once again clearly recognize, believe, and eagerly practice it. If within the sect there is no one with the actual experience of realizing the Way, and the *Shōbōgenzō* is dropped down to the level of thought and becomes a philosophy, I'm afraid Dōgen Zenji's Buddhadharma will vanish from the sect like clouds and mist.

Next he points out in detail how to realize the Way, to intimately perceive. "It is not like the reflection in a mirror, nor like the moon in the water." Here, by means of a meta-

phor, he clearly points out that realizing the way is completely
different from the realm of intellect and understanding.

The simile of the reflecting of an image in a mirror and
the reflecting of the moon in the water mean that the mirror
and the reflection, the water and the moon, are two separate
things that have become one, but the actual experience of enlightenment is a completely different matter. Therefore, even
if one can conceptually understand the principle of Zen or
intellectually comprehend the meaning of manifest absolute
reality *(genjōkōan),* that is not enlightenment.

Enlightenment means waking up to the world of oneness.
Unenlightened people look at everything dualistically: self and
other, subject and object, delusions and enlightenment, this
world and the Pure Land, unenlightened persons and buddhas, form and emptiness. Even if one tries to get rid of that
duality by mouthing the theory that "form is emptiness," the
seam of "is" remains. It's not the seamless stupa.[49]

The actual experience of enlightenment comes springing
forth in the realm of true oneness. And with that, one sometimes cries out in astonishment. One becomes aware that the
whole universe is just the single seamless stupa. It's not some
simplistic kind of thing like a reflection in a mirror.

"Mountains and rivers are not seen in a mirror."[50] It's not
that mountains, rivers, and the earth are reflected in one's
mind-mirror. That's okay when we are using metaphors for
thought and consciousness. But what we are speaking of now
is the realm of the actual experience of enlightenment. The
self is the mountains, rivers, and earth; the self is the sun and
moon and the stars.[51]

> The great earth has not
> A single lick of soil;
> New Year's first smile.[52]

"Not another person in the whole universe." One side is all there is, without a second or a third to be found anywhere. If one calls this subject, everything is subject and that's all. There is no object anywhere. It's the true mind-only.[53] It's snatching away the objective world but not the person. If one calls this object, everything is object and that's all. There is no subject anywhere. It's snatching away the person but not the objective world. It's the true matter-only. Whichever one you say, only the label changes and it is the same thing. While Dōgen Zenji calls this completely self, he also calls it completely other. It's all self. It's all other. This is the meaning of "when one side is realized the other side is dark." This is also called "one side exhausts everything." It's the whole thing, being complete with one, exhausting everything with one.

To study the Buddha way is to study oneself. To study one-
self is to forget oneself. To forget oneself is to be enlightened
by the myriad dharmas. To be enlightened by the myriad
dharmas is to bring about the dropping away of body and
mind of both oneself and others. The traces of enlighten-
ment come to an end, and this traceless enlightenment is
continued endlessly.

8

I N this section Dōgen Zenji painstakingly shows the sequential order in realizing the way. The first step in that
is, "To study the Buddha way is to study oneself." As I
always say, the Buddha way does not mean to look out at
the phenomenal world and intellectualize, saying, "That is
buddha-nature," "That is the dharma body," "That is the
manifestation of the truth." And to call that examining the
self! "What is your own original face?" "What was your self
before your parents were born?"[54] To practice turning one's
illumination within in this manner is the Buddha way. To identify the original self is the Buddha way.

"To study the Buddha way is to study oneself." To study
oneself what must one endeavor to do? What is essential is to
throw away one's own views and oneself. To throw away all
one's acquired affectations, which are the knowledge and experience accumulated since birth, to become a pure white
sheet of paper, and to bring oneself into accord with the
teachings of the buddhas and ancestors—that's the important
thing. While carrying around such things as "my ideas" and

"my opinions," one absolutely cannot attain the Buddha way. The Buddha way is the way of returning to one's intrinsic nature itself; how can one awaken to one's intrinsic nature when one is deluded by acquired affectations? "To forget oneself" is not to fall victim to amnesia. It's to throw away all former knowledge and views and to become a pure white sheet of paper. That's "to forget oneself." Dōgen Zenji is referring to this state in which one has forgotten oneself when he says, "To forget oneself is to be enlightened by the myriad dharmas."

"The myriad dharmas" means all dharmas. All dharmas are everything. Everything is the Buddha way. All dharmas are the Buddha-dharma. They are one's intrinsic nature itself. To completely discard one's own views and oneself, and then, moved by one's intrinsic nature itself, to carry out the activities of daily life as one's intrinsic nature—going out and returning home, getting dressed, eating and drinking, defecating and urinating—that is "to be enlightened by the myriad dharmas." That is the actualization of enlightenment, the full manifestation of original enlightenment, the full manifestation of the absolute nature. It's the *mani* jewel of original enlightenment. The *mani* jewel is the wish-fulfilling jewel. Whether one realizes it or not, that's how it is.

"The treasure house spontaneously opens and one receives and uses it freely."[55] This is the living form of "just sitting." In other words, just living, living as a pure white sheet of paper. This is the meaning of "being one single piece throughout the twenty-four hours of the day."[56] This is maintaining right mindfulness.[57] It's manifesting the buddha-seal in the three activities.[58] Whether properly sitting in *samadhi,* walking in *samadhi,* or conducting one's affairs in *samadhi,* the entire phenomenal world becomes the buddha-seal. All space without exception becomes enlightenment. Actually, there is no becoming or not becoming. It's always been that way. But unenlightened people are not at all able to forget themselves. In other words, since they can't become a pure white sheet of paper, Dōgen Zenji emphasizes just sitting, saying in the *Bendōwa,* "If a person for even one moment manifests the buddha-seal in the three activities, when properly sitting in *samadhi,* the whole phenomenal world becomes the buddha-seal, all space without exception becomes enlightenment." This is the meaning of "practicing the way with the beginner's mind is the whole body of original enlightenment."[59] It's also the meaning of "since it is the enlightenment of practice, en-lightenment is endless; since it is the practice of enlighten-ment, practice is beginningless."[60] It's also called "practice and enlightenment are one," and "original enlightenment and marvelous practice."[61] Herein also lies the true spirit of the mind of resolved faith of a person embraced by Amida Buddha.[62]

The next sentence is Dōgen Zenji's deeper, clearer, more precise expression of the living form of being enlightened by the myriad dharmas. "To be enlightened by the myriad dhar-mas is to bring about the dropping away of body and mind of both oneself and others." "Dropping away body and mind" is an expression that possesses a venerable origin and history. It is from the time when Dōgen Zenji reached the point of breaking away the bottom of the last bucket of ignorance and exclaimed, "The great matter of a lifetime's search has ended here." Here he doesn't use the word enlightenment, but that's because the expression "dropping away body and mind" is sufficient. Also, it is easy to see the meaning since the expres-sion "traces of enlightenment" follows right afterward. The content of this thing called enlightenment, which the monks of the Soto sect hate, or rather fear, has appeared without the use of the word *enlightenment*.

Dōgen Zenji's sentences are brief and to the point, and also the style is elevated, so unless one with a clear dharma eye fleshes them out appropriately, lowers the style and rephrases them for a spoon-feeding, they won't be understood by beginners. To read and chew on the original texts as they are is best, but as a temporary foothold I'll add a little padding.

Now, completely throwing away all one's previous knowledge and views, becoming a pure white sheet of paper, and living the life of one's intrinsic nature—and even if one doesn't understand it, believing that this is the whole of original enlightenment, the actualization of enlightenment—so long as one single-mindedly and free from confusion continues just living, simply living, a life of *samadhi,* that is completely dropping away body and mind. When seen from the point of view of the buddhas and ancestors, the life of that person doesn't differ one bit from the buddhas and ancestors who had thoroughgoing great enlightenment. Therefore, coming into contact with some cause, one suddenly attains great enlightenment with the thought, "Now I see, I was fine just as I was." That is "being enlightened by the myriad dharmas." It was true for people of the past, and it is also true for those of the present day. In the Way there is no past or present. This is "hearing a sound and realizing the Way, seeing a form and illuminating the mind,"[63] "seeing one's nature and attaining buddhahood,"[64] and so on.

When one has attained great self-awakening, where are there such things as one's own body and mind, and the bodies and minds of others? There's not a bit of cloud to obstruct the eye. One clearly awakens to the fact that self and other were the dreams of an unenlightened person, subject and object were just instances of delusion. That is expressed as, "To be enlightened by the myriad dharmas is to bring about the dropping away of body and mind of both oneself and others." This is "thorough-going great enlightenment." And then the last step is sweeping up after enlightenment. Any knocking of enlightenment ought to done only after one has reached this place. Since many Zen teachers indiscriminately knock enlightenment right from the start, novice monks are quite happy to avoid the diligence and hard work that goes into seeking enlightenment and the basic way of all-out practice. Then those with good minds just become scholars, and in terms of meaning the sect is destroyed. Then what remains in the sect is only the empty shell of intellectualizing and the art of lecturing. In the end it leads to the mistaken idea that the Buddha-dharma of Eihei Dōgen and the Buddha-dharma of Rinzai are different. How do they read Dōgen Zenji's expression, "Though the five houses differ, they are just the one seal of the buddha mind."?[65] Rinzai and Soto only differ in their means and methods of teaching, in which they each have their own characteristics.

Look at the buddhas and ancestors from the past. Didn't they all seek enlightenment and exert themselves in practice? Didn't Dōgen Zenji risk his life and endure the hardships of traveling to China in seeking enlightenment? Then he clearly attained enlightenment and returned home. The content of that enlightenment is "there is not a single hair of Buddha-dharma," "the eyes are horizontal, the nose is vertical."[66] It's returning to one's original state. It's one's intrinsic nature itself. Dōgen Zenji absolutely did not return home as an unenlightened being, but rather, having completely dropped away the skin of ideas, concepts, perceptions, and beliefs, and having become nothing but the one reality.

Now, since everyone is seeing the dreams of the unenlightened, everyone must somehow realize sudden, great enlightenment at least once. From olden times there are only a handful of people who have attained thoroughgoing great enlightenment in a single experience. Usually one reaches great liberation only after attaining enlightenment upon enlightenment over and over again. But! When one has attained enlightenment, unless the traces of enlightenment have been wiped away it's not true enlightenment. When a lazy fellow wipes up, he use dirty water, and so traces of the wiping cloth remain streaked behind. They are the traces of having wiped up. With the traces remaining it would be so unsightly one couldn't let a guest in.

To give another analogy: In order to clean off the dirt of delusion it is necessary to use the soap of enlightenment. However, when the dirt has been removed then one rinses the clothes, and unless one gets the smell of the soap out completely they can't be worn. The dirty smell may be unpleasant, but so is the soapy smell. So then, traces of enlightenment coming to an end becomes an absolute necessity. Dogen Zenji expresses this as "the traces of enlightenment come to an end."

What does he mean by "traceless enlightenment is continued endlessly"? If, upon attaining thoroughgoing great enlightenment, one then goes on to put an end to the traces of enlightenment, and having completely removed their smell, returns to one's original self, is that enough? Far from it! It's what one does from there that's important. The reason is that since one has with great effort become the original buddha, from here the work of the buddha begins. Having become a buddha, if one doesn't do anything at all it's a dead Buddha-dharma. It's a false buddha. One must further attain enlightenment upon enlightenment. One must become a person who is deluded within delusion. Even after one has attained buddhahood it is usual to advance further. In the Buddha way there are no dead ends. It's the practice of enlightenment. Practice and enlightenment have no limit. That's the life of the buddha. Dōgen Zenji expresses this noble, profound spirit as "traceless enlightenment is continued endlessly."

When a person starts to search out the dharma, he separates   9
himself far from the dharma. When the dharma has already
been rightly transmitted in oneself, just then one is one's
original self.   🌿   🌿

THIS section sums up both the beginning of the practice of the Buddha way and the time of full accomplishment of the dharma, and it has the sense of having tied together everything up to this point.

Our seeking the dharma or aspiring to become a buddha is truly a great mistake. Aren't sentient beings originally buddhas? We're buddhas right from the start. Is there any use in becoming buddhas again on top of that? One doesn't wash water with water or change gold into gold. If it is pure gold right from the start, is there any use in turning it into gold a second time? This is just like someone riding around on his ox looking for his ox.[67]

"Where are you going on your ox?"

"Oh, yes, I'm going to look for my ox."

"If it's your ox you're looking for, aren't you riding on it?"

"Ah! So I am."

See, having noticed that he was on it is enlightenment. This is a kind of silly thing, but there is not even one unenlightened person who knows that sentient beings are originally buddhas. Even Shakyamuni, until he became enlightened with a single glance at the morning star, did not know that at all. However, feeling no sense of responsibility, today we only su-

perficially hear the words "sentient beings are originally buddhas,"[68] and though with that we might say we understand or
we believe it, that's a complete sham. One who is originally a
buddha again attaining enlightenment and becoming a buddha is like some sort of goblin who puts one head on top of
another. Don't all the patriarchs of the past without exception
clearly say so? However, those who say that you don't need
enlightenment are like fools who cut off the head and then
look for the tongue. This also has been declared by the ancient
ancestors. What do you think about it? If you're enlightened
it's no good; if you're not enlightened it's even worse. If you
don't break out in a cold sweat over this point, nothing will be
accomplished.

That's the "original fundamental dharma-nature, inherent
self-nature body." And yet, "Why do all buddhas in the three
worlds arouse the thought of enlightenment, practice, and attain the Way?" This is the first doubt that Dōgen Zenji came
up against. The sectarian scholars of today still haven't really
even come up against the first doubt Dōgen Zenji had when
he started seeking Zen. So it is appalling to hear them say
"practice and enlightenment are one." For this reason, they
cannot at all see such things as the inner dynamics of Dōgen
Zenji immediately seeing his true nature when Eisai responded to him using Nan-ch'uan's words, "All buddhas in
the three worlds do not know of its existence. The dumb
beasts, on the other hand, know of its existence."[69] Here, taking Nan-ch'uan's words as live words, it is okay to express it
in simple Japanese, but for a person without the ability to accept it, even if you tell him, it's no good because he can't
accept it. Even though you throw the ball, if the catcher is
lousy it's useless. In the case of a person who has seen to the
bottom of his true nature, he should be able to accept Nan-

ch'uan's live words in proportion to his strength. To sum it up, it is something to investigate in the *dokusan* room. Explanations of words and phrases are things beginners ask about. They are not difficult even if asked about in public. You can even learn that by looking in a Zen dictionary. A real Zen monk in *sanzen (dokusan)* grasps the subtle meaning that is outside of the words from a single question and a single answer. So a Zen *mondō* is not a verbal exchange. It demands actual experience. Therefore we need *dokusan*.

Now those people in the sect who hate *kenshō*, who are afraid of *kenshō* (having guided them this way is the fault of their superiors) should inquire deeply into the causality discussed in this section. Regarding the above causality, Dōgen Zenji later, on Mount T'ien-t'ung, told Eisai Zenji's successor Myōzen, "I suddenly awakened and was covered with a cold sweat from head to foot." Those who have the actual experience of *kenshō* will nod their heads in assent saying, "I see, of course." At that time Myōzen affirmed that wholeheartedly, and, writing a verse, verified it. This verified the fact of Dōgen Zenji having seen his true nature.

After Eisai Zenji's death, Dōgen Zenji intimately studied the Rinzai style of koan Zen with Master Myōzen at Kenninji in Kyoto for nine years. After that he went over to China and, meeting the head cook of the monastery on Mount Yu-wang on a boat in Ching-yüan province, asked, "Why is it that although you are an old man, you are employed with the busy work of the head cook and not inquiring into the *watō* (koans) of the ancient ancestors?"[70] Even from looking at this, one can see that at Kenninji he was mainly doing koan Zen and it seems that he went to China when that study was finished. So, in China he was mainly doing *shikantaza*. However, I have never yet heard that Dōgen Zenji said that these nine years of koan Zen study at Kenninji were useless. Considering this, those of the Soto sect have no right to speak ill of koan Zen. Of course, because there are abuses in koan Zen, there must be a great deal of correction. At the same time, present-day *shikantaza* is in need of great reform in the same way as koan Zen.

"When the dharma has already been rightly transmitted in oneself, just then one is one's original self." Speaking in terms of the original self, searching out the dharma is a mistake. But this mistake is a mistake we must knowingly make. It is even said, "We make the mistake because we know." Why? Because a buddha, seeing the dreams of an unenlightened person, reacts to them. So, somehow he must open his eyes. Even the master of a wealthy house, if he dreams he is a beggar, reacts, saying, "I'm hungry, I'm hungry," and breaks out in a cold sweat.[71] If he doesn't somehow awaken to the fact that he is the master of a wealthy house, he can't get either fulfillment or peace of mind. So, the master of a wealthy house has to make strenuous efforts in order to awaken to the fact that he is the master of a wealthy house. That also is an excellent way to use zazen. Therefore, even using zazen as a means to realization is definitely not a bad thing. Just sitting by itself is not everything.

The great master Shih-t'ou Hsi-ch'ien said: "My sect does not argue about diligence and concentration but simply opens up the Buddha wisdom."[72] That's what's important. Zazen that ignores the opening up of the Buddha's wisdom is the defiled Zen of the Hinayana and unenlightened persons. However, the use of zazen as a means to enlightenment is only a tiny part. The rightly transmitted zazen of the buddhas and ancestors is the actual manifestation and actual practice of enlightenment. It is the Buddha's practice. It's practicing buddha. It's sitting buddha. And yet, that only becomes clear after having realization. Up until realization, one is only sitting with the faith that zazen is the practice of the Buddha. If that faith is weak, your zazen won't continue. Look at the monks of the Soto sect. They say that zazen is the practice of the Buddha. But do they ever do zazen?

"When the dharma has already been rightly transmitted in oneself," is thoroughgoing great enlightenment. Thoroughgoing great enlightenment is awakening to your original self. "This dharma is abundantly endowed in each person."[73] That is verified by practice. Therefore, "if it is not practiced, it won't be manifest; if it is not realized, it won't be attained." Even though we say "attained," it is not that we attain anything that is especially different. It is just important that we recognize that "the eyes are horizontal and the nose is vertical"[74] and are no longer deceived by other people. But, "the eyes are horizontal and the nose is vertical" as spoken by the average sect scholar is a downright sham. It's deluded views and deluded feelings. Therefore, it is nothing but being deceived by other people. "Don't be deceived by other people" does not refer to ordinary people. It means no longer being deceived even by all buddhas in the three worlds. The sect scholars are all deceived by the Buddha's sutras and the ancestor's records. Isn't that so? The true "eyes are horizontal, nose is vertical" is advice given after thoroughly penetrating the emptiness of eye, ear, nose, tongue, body, and mind, and clearly seeing the emptiness of all five *skandhas*.[75]

The Buddha-dharma is definitely something that is rightly transmitted. While right transmission is also called single transmission, it is called the transmission of no transmission, too. It's no transmission because there is nothing to be given and received. It wasn't necessary to receive even a bit of snot from the buddhas and ancestors. Only when one fully awakens to the fact that right from the start she has been lacking nothing at all, and gets the okay from her teacher, is it right transmission. Self-certification is no good. This is what is meant by "a pine rightly transmits to a pine; a bamboo rightly transmits to a bamboo."[76] Even though a plum tree may arbitrarily call itself a pine, that won't pass.

Therefore, first of all seek the dharma; seek a true teacher; ardently seeking, diligently advance in practice; attain thoroughgoing great enlightenment; and obtain certification from a teacher who has right transmission. Only then can it be said that one is immediately one's original self. That's returning to one's original self. That's becoming a true person.

If a person, when he is riding along in a boat, looks around and sees the shore, he mistakenly thinks that the bank is moving. But if he looks directly at the boat, he discovers that it is the boat that is moving along. Likewise, with confused thoughts about body and mind, holding to discrimination of the myriad dharmas, one mistakenly thinks his own mind and nature are permanent. If, intimately engaged in daily activities, one returns to right here, the principle that the myriad dharmas have no self is clear.

F R O M here Dōgen Zenji warns us against the view that the mind is permanent and only phenomenal appearances perish, and he points out the fact that the myriad dharmas are without self. The view of permanence of the mind and the perishing of phenomenal appearances, to state it simply, is the view that the body changes and passes away, but the spirit eternally abides unchanging. It is a view that is generally easy for those of a simple faith to fall into. The metaphor "a person, when he is riding in a boat" means just what it says and can be understood by anybody.

This metaphor is cited from the passage in the *Sutra of Perfect Enlightenment*,[77] which says, It is like "The moon moving when the clouds pass quickly, and the shore moving when a boat moves along."

"With confused thoughts about body and mind, holding to discrimination of the various dharmas, one mistakenly thinks his own mind and nature are permanent." An unenlightened person is completely confused about body and mind. As long as one has not clearly seen that the five *skandha*s are all empty,[78] no matter how great a scholar he may be, he is confused about body and mind. As a result he falls either into a view of permanence or a view of annihilation. Many people of a simplistic faith fall into a view of permanence. Many second-rate scientists fall into a view of annihilation. Here Dōgen Zenji especially warns against a view of permanence. A view of permanence is considering there to be a single, permanent, guiding self; considering there to be a fixed, unchanging soul; thinking that the self actually exists. Unenlightened people have the karmic illness of considering whatever they attach themselves to to have a self. If they make a group, they consider the group to have a self. If they attach themselves to the nation, they consider the nation to have a self. You would hardly think that there was a self in the planet, but if the world were to become completely unified and there were such a thing as a world-state, perhaps they would come to believe in a world-self.

The largest self that unenlightened people falsely believe in is the cosmic self. That's what it is when you think there is something that creates the universe, governs the universe, and provides for the universe. It seems that in India from ancient times that's what they have been calling Brahma heaven. In China they call it heaven or the will of heaven. It seems that they made conforming with that the basis of their teaching. I think that it is arising from this that we have such expressions as "heaven has put virtue in me," "enjoying the will of heaven, I have no further doubts," and "the will of heaven is called the nature of things. Conforming to the nature of things is called the Way. Cultivating the Way is called the teaching."

"The Buddha way is no-self." The one who thoroughly

realized that all things are without self was Shakyamuni Buddha. "The myriad teachings return to the one" is also fine, but if Buddhism compromises with religions that have a false belief in the self, it is no longer Buddhism at all. But then, if those religions other than Buddhism return to no-self, the bases of those religions will disappear, and those religions will be changed into something completely different. However, since there can only be one truth, I think that when the wisdom of human beings advances, one way or another they'll become one.

In recent times the ones who, comparatively speaking, are least inclined toward a false belief in self are the scientists. But I'm quite afraid that if they make one false step, they will fall into a view of nihilism. By no means do scientists think that body and mind exist separately, but they are liable to regard the body as important and neglect the mind. Western medicine up until now has been treating people from that standpoint. In contrast, it seems that the Eastern medical tradition has emphasized the mind since long ago. The expression, "illness originates in the spirit (*ki*)," is a common one. Even the word for sickness (*byōki*) means illness (*byō*) of the spirit (*ki*)." I hear that even in Western medicine they have lately come to regard the mind as important.

Of course it's confused thinking to consider mind and body as existing separately, but attaching greater or lesser importance to the mind or the body, after all, is also confused thinking. So, if you think that a fixed body or mind exists for even one minute, that is also confused thinking. When one thinks about everything with this kind of confused thinking as the basis, she makes the mistake of thinking that only the body changes, arises, and passes away and mentally depicts something like a spirit or a self that is eternally abiding and unchanging. This is the way ordinary people think. From there, the theory of the undying soul also emerges. So then, on the one hand is the fact that Buddhism stresses that there is no God and no soul, and yet she thinks that Buddhism is something that believes in an unchanging soul.

Thus it is necessary to examine the content of both of these views very, very well, but, since that gets rather lengthy, here I will abreviate it. If you falsely consider there to be a self, you fall into the mistake of a view of permanence, and if you think that at the time of death the individual personality returns to nothing, that is a view of annihilation, which is also a mistake. This is not at all just a matter of whether or not a soul remains after death. Rather, the important question is whether or not a fixed, unchanging self, called a soul, really exists right now in the living body and mind.

It seems the fact that the body is changing moment by moment could be understood by anyone, but, not knowing if it is the spirit or what, people can't help thinking that there is some fixed, unchanging thing called me. When they try to find out exactly what that "me" is, they don't understand its true character at all. This thing called me doesn't seem to be just the body, nor does it seem to be just the mind, nor does it seem to be a combination of body and mind. Yet it doesn't seem to be something apart from mind and body. Still, it doesn't seem to be body-and-mind itself either. It doesn't seem funny to say "my body," "my spirit," or "my spirit and flesh," so this thing called me seems to be that which possesses both body and spirit. Thinking that that kind of "me" actually exists from birth to death is the ordinary consciousness of everyone. So then, every one of us has much pain and difficulty throughout our lives because of that "me," and then it causes us to worry about the distant future: "What will happen to me after I die?"

However, Dōgen Zenji declares that believing in that "me" is confused thinking about body and mind. In the ears of unenlightened people, it's like a clap of thunder in a clear sky. But since that's the truth, it can't be helped. Penetrating this truth is the Buddha-dharma. From the beginning this thing called self is only a concept without any actual substance. It is like the horns of a hare or a turtle's fur. The horns of a hare or a turtle's fur can be depicted conceptually, expressed in words, and so on, but the actual thing does not exist. In exactly the same way, what we call myself is only an idea with no actual entity. So, it's confused thinking, it's a delusion. Deceived by this deluded, confused thinking, we blindly pursue desires and heedlessly fight, and so on, continuing to suffer for a whole lifetime, until in the end it even leads to a world war. Thus, an "unenlightened person" means an existence without compassion. The buddhas and ancestors, seeing our suffering and being unable to bear it, earnestly expound the dharma, saying, "Quickly realize no-self; awaken to the fact of no-self."

"If, intimately engaged in daily activities, one returns to right here, the principle that the myriad dharmas have no self is clear."

"Daily activities" means our everyday activities. But it's not the activities of an unenlightened person. Here it means the activities of a person of the Way. It is the activities of a practitioner. Therefore, it is the activities of practicing the Buddha way. What does it mean to be intimately engaged and to return to right here? You are not "intimate" by levels of understanding or intellectual study. Therefore, it is no good if you don't penetrate Zen and practice the Way; truly penetrate it and truly investigate it thoroughly. Truly penetrating and truly investigating it thoroughly—that's what "intimate" means. So then, returning to right here is a necessity.

As for "right here," don't fret, thinking it is difficult. If we say it simply, it's "this." That's a way of saying it without giving it a name. What is "this"? It is one's own original face. Therefore, returning to right here is returning to "this." In other words, it means to fully realize and penetrate one's own original face. If you do that, "the principle that the myriad dharmas have no self is clear." Though it says principle, it is not just a matter of theory.[79] In the Buddha-dharma, phenomenal existence and principle are never separate. Therefore, if we say "principle," phenomenal existence is perfectly included in that. So then, "the principle that the myriad dharmas have no self" refers to the myriad dharmas, all dharmas, every dharma. There are no exceptions. This makes clear the fact that both oneself and everything in the universe are completely without self. Then, for the first time, one fully penetrates the fact that there is no God and no soul. Without realizing that, one can never fully penetrate Zen. But if you realize it and stop there, you will fall into a view of nihilism.

Among present-day teachers, one occasionally sees some who have fallen into a view of nihilism. A little bit of realization is a dangerous thing. However, it is a place one must pass through at some point. It is no good to be afraid of satori because it is dangerous. Why? Because just intellectually understanding the theory of no-self is like knowing what is in another person's wallet. Even though you may know exactly what is in it, that doesn't make a single penny of it yours. You absolutely cannot grasp the fact of no-self with intellectual studies. No matter how impressed you are upon hearing that our consciousness and body arise and perish 6,400,099,980 times a day[80]—even though you exclaim your understanding, saying, "Now I see,"—that can't even begin to touch the fact of no-self. Without penetrating the fact of no-self, you don't know the flavor of emptiness.

> The fruit of the pear tree
> And the pear
> Are the one fruit of this tree.
> In eating it,
> There are not two tastes.[81]

Unless you actually eat it and see, the pear's taste is something you will never get to know. Do you know the taste of a pear just by studying it intellectually and theoretically? If you could fill your belly like that, it would very economical!

Firewood becomes ash. It does not turn into firewood **11**
again. But, we should not hold to the view that the ash is
after and the firewood is before. Know that firewood abides
in its dharma position as firewood and has its past and
future. Though it has its past and future, it cuts off past and
future. Ash is in its dharma position as ash and has its past
and future. Just as this firewood, after it has become ash,
does not turn into firewood again, so a person, after death,
does not take rebirth.[82] *Therefore, we do not say that life*
becomes death. This is the established way of the Buddha-
dharma. For this reason it is called unborn. Death does not
become life. This is the established buddha-turning of the
dharma wheel. For this reason it is called undying. Life is
its own time. Death is its own time. For example, it is
like winter and spring. We don't think that winter becomes
spring. We don't say that spring becomes summer.

T HIS section explains the problem of life and death
more minutely, more clearly, and it examines the
central point that all dharmas are without self in
terms of time. It thoroughly demolishes the deluded, ordinary views of the unenlightened person for us,
including of course, the false view that mind is permanent and
only phenomenal appearances perish. As a result, if we misunderstand, there is a great danger of falling into a view of annihilation, so it calls for special caution. The phrase "firewood
becomes ash" is accommodated language. The words are ar-

ranged in a way that will accord with the feelings of unenlightened people. In other words, "firewood becomes ash" is written in a way that plays up to the feelings of unenlightened people, but Dōgen Zenji's true intention is to say, "Firewood does not become ash."

"It does not turn into firewood again," can also be grasped by ordinary consciousness, but that contains the possibility of a fearful pitfall. This is where Dōgen Zenji holds out a piece of candy and catches us.

"But we should not hold to the view that the ash is after and the firewood is before." There! You're caught, and it will be a terrible fate for you! No, actually, it's a blessing. It thoroughly destroys the sickness of the ordinary consciousness of the unenlightened person. We think that it is a matter of course that since the firewood turned into ash, we see the ash as after and the firewood as before. However, that is the illness of ordinary consciousness. It's the upside-down delusion of the unenlightened person. It goes without saying that the ash does not become firewood, but also, the firewood absolutely does not become ash. This is not a theory. It is a reality. Because some people try to assert it as a theory, they end up with a load of difficult words. They simply depict such things as impermanence, no-self, or emptiness in their heads, and since that theory is merely something that they've fabricated out of concepts, the impermanence, no-self, or emptiness that those people speak of is completely false. So, if one concretely thrusts before them the reality of impermanence, the reality of no-self, and the reality of emptiness, it leaves them bewildered.

To say it more completely, right from the start neither the firewood nor the ashes, neither I nor you exists anywhere. Viewing them as existing is the delusion of an unenlightened person. So, for a person who has clearly awakened to the fact that it is a delusion, it is fine to say either that everything exists or that nothing exists. Because whichever he says, it's really not so! How much more is it the case that "as for the four phrases of a deluded person, all four phrases are false." The four phrases are "exist," "don't exist," "both," and "neither."[83] It means that whatever an unenlightened person says, it is wrong. "As for the four phrases of an enlightened person, all four phrases are true." With an enlightened person, whatever he says is unerring.

All existence is like a dream, a phantasm, a reflection. Even though you're seeing it and touching it, it has no actual substance. I'll give you a concrete example. An electric news screen is like that. It has a lot of light bulbs and shows letters by lighting some of them up. It seems to make those letters flow, and informs you of the news at night. When you look at it from afar, it certainly seems as though the letters are flowing, but when you go up close and look at it, it is just some light bulbs going on and off, and there is not a single flowing letter. In the same way as that, everything in the universe seeming to exist and seeming to be active is completely untrue. That is the delusion common to everyone. That is why the Buddha calls us sentient beings with upside-down delusions.

This time I'll give myself as a concrete example. Suppose that just now I walked from my study to my living room. In truth, myself, the study, and the living room are without any actual substance, like the moon in the water. Setting that aside for a moment, considering it to be the same "me" that has gone from the study to the living room is the ordinary human consciousness. And yet, that is what is called the upside-down delusion of the unenlightened person. Actually, in the space of a single day, myself, the study, the living room, and the whole universe are all repeating a complete change about 6,400,099,980 times. Because of that, the existence we call me is one that is not provided with even the time it takes to make a single step, it is an existence that has almost no duration. An unlimited alternation of completely different persons is continued with a fearful speed. One who is under the false impression that it is the same human is an unenlightened person. Everything in the universe is like that. *The Song of the Enlightened Way* sings this as "all phenomena are impermanent, and completely empty. This is the great perfect awakening of the Tathagatas."[84] Therefore, thinking that a baby becomes a child, a child becomes an adolescent, an adolescent becomes a person in the prime of life, a person in the prime of life becomes an old person, and an old person dies— thinking that that is the same person—is the ordinary consciousness of a human being, and is an awful delusion that goes against reality. One must realize that in a single day one passes through this change about six and a half billion times. If it were explaining only this, I don't think this section would be particularly hard to understand. But it cuts off the ground, it cuts off position, it cuts off everything. It cuts off past and future. If we speak of the aspect of the continuity of the past and the present, then cause and effect in the three worlds of past, present, and future, and the wheel of the six destinies come up, but that is hidden in the interior. Dōgen Zenji takes that up in such fascicles of the *Shōbōgenzō* as "The Karma of the Three Times."

"Know that firewood abides in its dharma position as firewood[85] and has its past and future. Though it has its past and future, it cuts off past and future." Here Dōgen Zenji teaches in a way that plays up to the feelings of us unenlightened people. If it were said with no restraint, it wouldn't get through to unenlightened people at all. Shall we try saying it without any restraint?

"Know that firewood is not firewood. There is not a moment for it to abide in its dharma position as firewood. It has no past or future. Past and future are cut off." If one is a person who has seen to the bottom of his true nature, and was able to grasp the explanation of the previous step, he should be able to accept it even if the point is made rather directly like this.

"Ash is in its dharma position as ash and has its past and future." The lines that implicitly follow this, "Though it has its past and future, it cuts off past and future," are omitted. Of course, the spirit is the same as before. "Ash is not ash. There is not a moment for it to abide in its dharma position as ash. It has no past and future. Past and future are cut off."

"Just as this firewood, after it has become ash, does not turn into firewood again, so a person, after death, does not take rebirth." Dōgen Zenji has really chewed this one up well for us before feeding it to us. Those who blindly believe that there is a soul that changes bodies, changes its lodging, and is reborn, will be very surprised here. Still, that view is much more harmless than those who shallowly misunderstand this kind of important teaching and mistakenly consider the "Karma of the Three Times," "Refuge in the Three Treasures" and "Mind of the Way" fascicles of the *Shōbōgenzō* to be teachings based on expediency [for those of lesser capacity]. Thus they ignore birth and death, and past and present, and totally fall into the non-Buddhist view of annihilation. These days you sometimes see people who have that kind of understanding and are called Roshi. It sends a chill down my spine. Children shouldn't be allowed to play with the famed swords of Masamune.[86] To tell the truth, the eternalist view is much closer to reality than the nihilist view.

We shouldn't let them get away with saying that finally this *Genjōkōan* fascicle shows only one side of reality. No matter how good an orator one is, he cannot express the two sides of affirmation and negation at the same time. "Karma of the Three Times" and those other fascicles have the same value. Both are the complete Treasury of the True Dharma Eye. That is why I say that those young bodhisattvas who are practicing the Way of Zen should respectfully read the *Shōbōgenzō* beginning with whatever sections seem readily understandable to them.

This section also is written in a manner in which each side expresses both sides, although only half of it is shown on the surface. If we express the other half, it's like this: "Firewood has not a moment in which to become ash. Thus, firewood does not turn to ash. Just as firewood does not turn to ash, a person's life does not become death."

For evidence that this is an abbreviated expression, we can look at the next line. "Therefore, we do not say that life becomes death. This is the established way of the Buddhadharma." The living do not die. Living things absolutely do not die. Only dying things die. It's not a joke. It's true. As long as you're alive, you won't die, so don't worry. When you die you won't be alive, so don't worry about that either. Even when you hear it said like this, can you still not find peace of mind? Both life and death are the liberating teaching that is difficult to encounter. No matter how you dress it up, life and death can never come together. Far from it! Since from the first there is nothing that dies, how could there be a way in which it dies?

"Until now, as I thought it meant other persons, it was

okay, but the fact it's me who will die, I cannot bear." Of course this is a deluded view. This is said to be a corny joke by someone from Szechwan province or somewhere, but being able to make even one joke when facing death is not bad. And it's nothing to be all that impressed with either. My "In Praise of the *Shushōgi*"[87] contains the following poem.

> Researching in atomic science
> It finally has dawned,
> That what I took for matter
> Is only motion's form.
> More surprising yet, indeed,
> Three thousand years before,
> Buddha's great wisdom: cause and effect
> With no one at its core.
> So altogether, everyone,
> Be not afraid of death;
> Give up seeking something that
> Will yield up the last breath.
> If you see there to be
> Any I to die,
> It merely is the dream
> Of a deluded eye.

Then, skipping over the line, "For this reason it is called unborn," next we come to, "Death does not become life. This is the established buddha-turning of the dharma wheel." It goes without saying that this is parallel to what comes before. The phrase "the established buddha-turning of the dharma wheel" is what we would call a truly refined and marvelous one, but if we said that to Dōgen Zenji, he might scold us for praising him excessively. It may have been a phrase that Dōgen Zenji turned effortlessly, but it has an indescribably subtle flavor. Of course it has the same meaning as "the established way of the Buddha-dharma," which comes before it.

Since death not becoming life has been fully explained, there should be no need to go into it again. But we should inquire deeply into the fact that, like the phrases that come before and after, we have the parallel construction of "for this reason it is called unborn," and "for this reason it is called undying." It has an especially subtle flavor. This is also written so that each side expresses both sides. He has divided up the whole and abridged it so that he gives only half of it in each part. That arrangement of phrases is overflowing with Dōgen Zenji's dharma strength and kindheartedness. Written in an unabbreviated form, it would read like this: "We do not say that life becomes death. This is the established way of the Buddha-dharma. For this reason we say, 'Unborn, undying.' Death does not become life. This is the established buddha-turning of the dharma wheel. For this reason we say, 'Undying, unborn.' "

Simply stated, it's like this: "Life does not become death and death does not become life. Therefore although things appear to be born and to die, there is nothing to be born or to die." There's nothing difficult about it. The problem is just whether or not one can accept this fact, saying, "Oh, I see. That's the way it is." It's not enough to understand it theoretically. No matter how well you understand it in theory, it's not enough. It's not some kind of study of principles.[88] It is essential to actually open your eyes. That's why Dōgen Zenji took care here to use expressions that at first glance appear illogical. Therefore, because the meaning of the two words *unborn* and *undying* is the same, it doesn't matter which one is chosen. However, Dōgen Zenji was probably concerned about the possibility that, later, some within his dharma lineage would degenerate into scholastics. He was probably taking precautions by putting "unborn" together with "we do not say that life becomes death," and "undying" together with "death does not become life." Then comes, "Life is its own time. Death is its own time." Finally we've come to the line that caps off this section of the text. What comes after it adds power to the sentence. This expression can be explained by anybody. The meaning is obvious, and can probably be understood even without an explanation. Especially since it is followed by the simile of the seasons, anybody should be able to understand it intellectually. Scholastics think that it's good enough if you understand it, but as I've said time and time again, there is a big difference between having understood it in your head and having grasped the reality of it. Without having grasped the reality of life and death each being its own time, you cannot have true peace of mind.

Let's take a look at the koan, "Tao-wu's Condolence Call," case 55 in the *Blue Cliff Record*.[89] If it were good enough just to understand, Master Tao-wu would have given some kind of explanation. However, since in the end understanding doesn't help, he taught with the utmost kindness, saying, "I won't say! I won't say!"

So, then, if we remove the accommodated language and lay bare the essential meaning, this section would read as follows: "Not only does ash not become firewood, but firewood does not become ash either. Firewood has not a moment to abide in its dharma position as firewood. It cuts off past and future. Ash also is without a moment to abide in its dharma position as ash. Past and future are cut off. Not only does a person not take rebirth after dying, but neither does a person's life lead to death. That life does not become death and death does not become life is the established teaching of Buddha-dharma. For this reason we say, 'unborn and undying.' Life is its own time. Death is its own time. For example, it is like winter and spring. We don't think that winter becomes spring. We don't say that spring becomes summer."

Above is the spirit of what Dōgen Zenji is saying, but since he employs accommodated language, his explanation is a gentle one. So then, once you read it with an understanding of the meaning, there is nothing difficult about it at all. And yet, to actually experience the reality of it is no easy thing to do.

It seems that in order to liberate people from eternalistic views, Dōgen Zenji was forced to speak as he does above. Thus, you should use these words to completely discard the theory of an imperishable soul that contains the assertion of a substantial self. But don't go overboard and fall into a nihilist view. Right View, which falls into neither nihilism nor eternalism, is something that appears only after one has had a realization. That then forms the foundation of the practice of the Buddha way. That's why Right View comes first on the Noble Eightfold Path.

A person getting enlightened is like the moon reflecting in the water. The moon does not get wet, the water is not disturbed. Though it is a great expanse of light, it reflects in a little bit of water; the whole moon and the whole sky reflect even in the dew on the grass; they reflect even in a single drop of water. Enlightenment not disturbing the person is like the moon not piercing the water. A person not obstructing enlightenment is like the dewdrop not obstructing the heavens. The depth is the measure of the height. As for the length or brevity of the time [of the reflection], one ought to examine whether the water is large or small and discern whether the sky and moon are wide or narrow.

12

I N this section Dōgen Zenji points out the state of affairs when we have an experience of realization. Earlier in the *Genjōkōan*, Dōgen says, "In mustering the whole body and mind and seeing forms, in mustering the whole body and mind and hearing sounds, they are intimately perceived; but it is not like the reflection in a mirror, nor like the moon in the water." Yet when we get to here he says: "A person getting enlightened is like the moon reflecting in the water." At first glance the former statement and the latter appear to contradict each other. New and old practitioners alike should take note that this is not the case. Here the metaphor of the water and the moon is being used differently, so it's just a matter of the language being the opposite.

The first phrase, "A person getting enlightened," can be

appreciated from both the standpoint of the original self and from the point of view of practice and enlightenment. In this section of the text the emphasis is placed on the side of practice and enlightenment. So then, first we have to clearly recognize the fact that there is a realization to be gained. It is not enough just to look at it from the intrinsic standpoint and say "we're originally enlightened." Dōgen Zenji teaches us that realization is, just as it says, "like the moon reflecting in the water." Comparing enlightenment to the moon and we human beings to water, he tells us that "the moon does not get wet, the water is not disturbed." On this point there are books that are thick with explanations about the water and the moon, but it's just a lot of chatter. We're not children and can understand the metaphor perfectly well from the text. However, what we have to do is to clarify what that means in relation to "a person getting enlightened."

"The moon does not get wet, the water is not disturbed" points to a state in which enlightenment and the person do not obstruct each other at all. Concretely speaking, first of all it indicates that anyone can become enlightened. It means one should not regard the wise as superior and the stupid as inferior, or prefer the clever to the dull. It means that when one exerts oneself single-mindedly, that is truly practicing the Way, that is the Buddha way. It also indicates that practice and realization are naturally undefiled. In other words, this is what is pointed out by the metaphor "the moon does not get wet, the water is not disturbed." To put it more simply it means that anyone can get enlightened, but even if you are enlightened you won't be especially different. You're the same person you were before. That's the moon not disturbing the water. It's ordinary. It's undefiled. Also, no matter what kind of water the moon of realization reflects in, it is not soiled. No matter who it is that is enlightened, whether a novice monk or an abbot, a scholar or an ignorant illiterate, a king or a beggar, the moon of enlightenment is something that can neither be wetted nor stained by the water of that person. No matter who it is that's enlightened, there is no change in the content of the enlightenment. Isn't that obvious? It's because you are opening your eyes to your own inherent nature. Can you have two or three inherent natures? "The dharma has only one vehicle, not two or three."[90]

"Though it is a great expanse of light, it reflects in a little bit of water. The whole moon and the whole sky reflect even in the dew on the grass; they reflect even in one drop of water." The light of the moon of enlightenment is vast. It is the inherent nature of the universe. Just as the vast light of that moon is refleced by the water in a vessel that is only one foot or one inch wide, our single-minded devotion allows this univeral inherent nature to be perfectly reflected and we have a sudden, great enlightenment.

"The whole moon and the whole sky reflect even in the dew on the grass; they reflect even in a single drop of water" extends the metaphor and adds emphasis to the spirit of what precedes it.

"Enlightenment not disturbing the person is like the moon not piercing the water. A person not obstructing enlightenment is like the dew drop not obstructing the heavens." Here, Dōgen Zenji shows us more clearly and in greater detail the spirit of the previous section. When the moon reflects in the water, it doesn't make a hole in the water. In the same way becoming enlightened does not mean that we stop being human.

Having a thoroughgoing great enlightenment does not mean we become something other than a human being, with-

out happiness and without troubles. After all "flowers fall
amid our longing and weeds spring up amid our antipathy."

> Though I thought I had cast away the world
> And was without self
> Snowy days are all the colder.[91]

So then, becoming enlightened, is one exactly the same as an
unenlightened person? If one is the same then there is no
need for enlightenment. From the standpoint of the original
self, that is of course true, but can we really be satisfied with
that, can we really have peace of mind? If anything appears to
be other than yourself, you absolutely cannot have peace of
mind.

Only when you are in favorable circumstances and your
good fortune goes along without a hitch do you seem to be
somewhat at ease, but that's not the real thing. It's really only
being drowned in favorable circumstances. How is it when
you are assailed by repeated misfortune and continual miser-
ies? Can you really stand as firm as a rock and be completely
at peace? When you are in the pits of hell and can still truly
know the wondrous joy of the Third Dhyana Heaven, then
you don't need to have a realization.[92] If that is not the case,
then you definitely need to have a thoroughgoing great enlightenment. These comments are made from the standpoint
of practice and enlightenment.

However, these days those in the Soto sect don't know
anything about this standpoint of practice and enlightenment.
They simply look at things only from the standpoint of the
original self and think that that is the whole of the Buddha-
dharma, so that standpoint of the original self also becomes
phony. Thereby they clutch onto a false Zen without practice

or realization, and mistake it for the Buddha-dharma with its original enlightenment and wondrous practice.

And then, even if they understand that the whole thing is meaningless without realization, they whimper, "For someone like me something like enlightenment is impossible." That's just what the followers like to hear. They heap glorious praise upon Zen, elevate it to a high place and then say, "We are ignorant people defiled by a deep accumulation of sins and can't do a single thing that is good, so all we can do is rely on the compassion of Amida Buddha." Thus they have a bargain sale on the peace of mind of those who are embraced by the Other Power and collect offerings.[93] Very good businessmen! Zen is straightforward and discards expedient means. It teaches that one must have direct realization.

In his *Precautions on Learning the Way*, Dōgen Zenji harshly criticizes attitudes such as those above: "What is the dharma that these people want, which is easy to understand and easy to practice? It is not the way of the world; neither is it the way of the Buddha. So then, we should call it the height of delusion of ignorant people."[94] So, don't make offerings. Zen is penniless. It's a way of poverty. But, impoverishing oneself, the Way is not impoverished.

That's the Way! Truly, anyone at all is certain to be able to attain enlightenment if he has the great determination Shakyamuni Buddha had when he said, "Until I attain enlightenment I will not stand up from this seat." "A person not obstructing enlightenment is like the dewdrop not obstructing the heavens." We think that we have a tiny little existence, like a drop of dew—though ignorant people mistakenly think so, each of us has the absolute existence of the I that swallows up the whole universe—so then the fact that we can be deeply enlightened is like a dewdrop reflecting the full moon and the vast sky but not hindering it in any way.

"The depth is the measure of the height. As for the length or brevity of the time of the reflection, one ought to examine whether the water is large or small and discern whether the sky and moon are wide or narrow." This wraps up this section. When it comes to enlightenment, there are a lot of people who fall into the one-sided view that all are the same and don't know that there are tremendous differences in clarity and depth. Realization itself is returning to one's inherent nature, and so there shouldn't be two or three different ones. But when we examine the extent to which one is able to return to that inherent nature, there are tremendous differences. That is what is called the clarity and depth of enlightenment.

Now I would like you to understand clearly that cause and effect are one. Hakuin Zenji's *Zazen wasan* says, "Open the gate of the oneness of cause and effect, don't think that there are two or three vehicles."[95] This is not the usual theory of cause and effect. The usual theory of cause and effect explains things from the standpoint of dependent origination in accord with causes and conditions. Here cause-and-effect is being shown from the standpoint of the true form of formlessness, which is without self and empty of its own nature. Therefore, when you understand the expression "since self-nature is no-nature, if you directly realize your self-nature, you have already departed from meaningless debates," the expression "open the gate of the oneness of cause and effect" directly shows us that all forms are the true form.

Now in this "oneness of cause and effect," cause-and-effect means that there are differences of clarity and depth in enlightenment. In other words, it points to the fact that there are levels in practice-enlightenment. Oneness means that the content of enlightenment is equal and without distinctions. In other words it points to the fact that there are no levels. Concretely speaking, this means that although there are tremendous differences in the clarity and depth of realization depending on the maturity of a person's practice, the content of realization itself is always one and the same. Levels are no-levels, no-levels are levels. This is the properly transmitted Zen of the buddhas and ancestors. In other words it is the properly transmitted Zen of Dōgen Zenji. This is the meaning of the teaching that there is only one vehicle, not two or three. However, there is a tendency for Rinzai Zen to present the Zen of levels on the surface with the Zen of no levels as its background, and for Soto Zen to present no-level Zen on the surface with the Zen of levels as its background. So then it seems that the Rinzai stream places emphasis on the Zen of levels and the Soto stream places emphasis on no-level Zen. Those who lack the dharma eye misperceive this. They think that Rinzai Zen is only the Zen of levels and bad-mouth it, calling it stepladder enlightenment, or else they mistake Soto Zen to be only no-level Zen that denies realization, and degrade Dōgen Zenji's properly transmitted Buddha-dharma, taking it to be intellectual Zen, conceptual Zen, or explanatory Zen.

If it falls into the side of the Zen of levels, or if it falls into the Zen of no-levels, it can never be the properly transmitted Zen of the buddhas and ancestors. In *Bendōwa*, "the practice of the beginner is the whole body of original enlightenment" is taught from the standpoint of no-levels, while "without practice it will not be manifest, without enlightenment it will not be attained," expressses the standpoint of levels.[96]

"The depth is the measure of the height." The deeper the water is, correspondingly the more deeply the height of the moon is reflected in the water. With this metaphor Dōgen

Zenji teaches us that the deeper one's practice is, the deeper, higher, brighter one's realization becomes. In other words, he clarifies the fact that in our practice-enlightenment there are unlimited depths. It goes without saying that he would not permit a blind-eyed Zen without practice and enlightenment; and warning us against being satisfied with a single feeble realization, he clarifies the fact that there are unlimited levels of practice and enlightenment.

"As for the length or brevity of the time [of the reflection], one ought to examine whether the water is large or small and discern whether the sky and moon are wide or narrow." Here, suddenly, the word *time* comes up, and it might seem as though he has suddenly taken off on a discussion of time, but that's not the case. This *time* is the "when" in "when all dharmas are the Buddha-dharma."[97] In short, it's the length or brevity of the time of one's practice of zazen. In other words it is the maturity or immaturity of practice.

In the practice of the Buddha way (and in fact it's the same with any "way"), maturity cannot simply be measured in length of time. There are some who go along lazily, some who make average effort, some who are truly ardent, and some who throw their whole life into it. If they practice for the same amount of time a great difference will emerge in the result, so it can't be measured merely in terms of time. Since understanding that is just a matter of common sense, he communicates the main point to us concisely with "the length or brevity of the time."

What does "examine whether the water is large or small" mean? "Large or small water" is a metaphor for the size, depth, and purity of our aspiration to practice the Buddha way as well as the length and ardor of our practice. In other words, it's a metaphor for the maturity of our practice. We should examine the maturity of our practice in order to distinguish its breadth and depth, and whether it is penetrating or not. Here the degree of one's enlightenment is compared with the breadth or narrowness of the sky and moon. "Eighteen great enlightenments, countless small enlightenments" is the expression of one of the ancients.[98] What this passage tells us is that people of the present day should also have this kind of experience.

Of course this also unfolds from the very first passage of the whole text, "When all dharmas are the Buddha-dharma, there are delusion and enlightenment," and is nothing but manifest absolute reality.

13

If the dharma has not yet fully come into one's body and mind, one thinks it is already sufficient. On the other hand, if the dharma fills one's body and mind, there is a sense of insufficiency. It is like going out in a boat in the middle of an ocean with no mountains. Looking in the four directions one only sees a circle; no distinguishing forms are seen. Nevertheless, this great ocean is neither a circle nor has directions. The wondrous features of this ocean that remain beyond our vision are inexhaustible. It is like a palace; it is like a jeweled necklace. It is just that, as far as my vision reaches for the time being, it appears to be a circle. The myriad dharmas are also just like that. Though they include all forms within and beyond the dusty world, clear seeing and understanding only reach as far as the power of our penetrating insight.

THERE is nothing difficult to understand in the text of this section. "Dharma," here, is the Buddha-dharma. It means the Buddha way. When in our body and mind we are not sufficiently possessed of the Buddha-dharma, and accordingly we cannot chew up the Buddha way sufficiently, we give rise to the deluded view that we have understood the Buddha-dharma fully. That's the disease of arrogance. The worst cases are the ones who become boastful with their first small glimpse of their true nature. That's why my revered teacher Daiun Shitsu [Harada Sōgaku Roshi] was especially stern in cautioning those who had had their first glimpse about this point. Further, when he had finished his test in the *dokusan* room, he repeatedly warned us about the disease of arrogance and told us how he himself had suffered from the disease of arrogance for seven or eight years. He taught us how much of a hindrance it is to both oneself and others in our progress in the Way, and how much it causes the brilliance of the Buddha way to be lost. He always urged great reflection upon this.

When you first see your true nature, you feel as though you have cut off the demon's head.[99] If you don't feel like that, you haven't really seen it. However, in being tested with koans after seeing your true nature, and getting stuck time and time again, you come to understand that it is not a demon's head nor even a mouse's head that you've gotten. Therefore those who think that their first shallow glimpse of their true nature is good enough and give up their study of the Way under a master are truly pitiable. Those who just catch a glimpse of one aspect of the dharma and then become lax will find that their insight completely vanishes again. The memory of seeing your true nature lasts for a while, but that memory is just a shadow, not the real thing. Therefore it's not realized in that person's character or his lifestyle. It's nothing more than giving rise to an arrogant, self-centered idea that one has realized his true nature.

As one proceeds to be tested in the *dokusan* room and continues going five hundred, a thousand, fifteen hundred times, she gradually comes to see the thread of the dharma. Of course, since going to dokusan with a half-baked teacher is a half-baked way of passing through koans, you shouldn't be satisfied no matter how many you pass, but there are some people who are satisfied with that. That's because those people do not truly have the mind that seeks the Way. Rather, they have some ill intent connected with reputation and profit, such as making a show of having done Zen or wanting to hurry up and become a Zen teacher for the sake of their own pride. That's why they can be satisfied with something that isn't real. It's only that kind of person who blindly rushes to pass through koans. Occasionally there are even people who come into *dokusan* five or six times even when it's not *sesshin*. When I refuse to allow that, they say they have misgivings about the dharma or that they regret their efforts. I've tried not refusing them, but the result is no good. The koans don't really become their own at all. The koan and the person's state are separate. So then, having done nothing but memorize the technique for handling the koan, they're all done with it. That has nothing to do with Zen, and we can say it is the ultimate abuse of koan Zen.

Therefore, koans are something that should be done thoroughly and unhurriedly while exerting oneself diligently in zazen. They are something that should be done with exactly the same feeling as a person who has been just sitting for ten, twenty, thirty years. Of course being lazy and just ambling along slowly is a most disgraceful thing, but it's no good to go to *dokusan* again and again in one period of zazen. That's just being rash. If you're chased out with a no over and over again on the same koan, that in itself amounts to the same thing as being taught indirectly, so in the end even when one passes the koan it has no real power. The ideal is to hit the bull's-eye with the first arrow, but it's not so easily done. So then for *dokusan*, you should sufficiently polish the koan and approach it prudently.

As the dharma gradually becomes clear, the fact that there is a dreadful gap between the dharma and one's own personality and way of life also becomes clear. So with a sense that "this is no good, no good, still no good," one comes to feel wretched about oneself. Of course on the one hand one gains self-confidence, but on the other hand one always has the feeling that something is lacking and somehow feels ill at ease no matter what he does. This is the basic condition for training. "If the dharma fills one's body and mind, there is a sense of insufficiency."

Next comes, "It is like going out in a boat in the middle of an ocean with no mountains. Looking in the four directions one only sees a circle; no distinguishing forms are seen." This tells us what Dōgen Zenji actually realized from his own experience, and the meaning is clear, so no explanation is necessary. Nor is one necessary for what follows, "Nevertheless, this great ocean is neither a circle nor has directions. The wondrous feature of this ocean that remain beyond our vision are inexhaustible.

"It is like a palace; it is like a jeweled necklace. It is just that, as far as my vision reaches for the time being, it appears to be a circle." This needs a little explanation. Of course it shows more concretely the spirit of "the wondrous features of the ocean that remain beyond our vision are inexhaustible," and here the "four views of a single body of water" is being quoted as an example. According to the fruits of one's past karma, the same water will appear to have different forms and will serve different functions. Humans see it as water and use it as water, but fish see it as a home and use it as a home. These two cases can be grasped with ordinary human perception, but the latter two cannot be understood by those suffering the illness of ordinary human consciousness.[100] It is said that what humans see as water, heavenly beings use as a jeweled necklace, and hungry ghosts see as bloody pus.

"The myriad dharmas are also just like that. Though they

include all forms within and beyond the dusty world, clear seeing and understanding only reach as far as the power of our penetrating insight." In this section the "myriad dharmas" has come up again. Up to here all the talk has been about the Buddha way, but it's not just limited to the Buddha way. Through the example of "the four views of a single body of water," Dōgen Zenji has called our attention to the fact that it is the same in the realm of all phenomena, which is called "the myriad dharmas," and that it's a terrible mistake to think that the world that is reflected in the mirror of a human being's karma is the whole of the world.

"Dusty" points to the world of an unenlightened person with its five desires and six dusts.[101] "Beyond" is a word used to indicate the Buddha-dharma. Both the world and that which is beyond the worldly are complex and multifaceted, profound and subtle; the myriad forms and circumstances are incalculable. You grasp them only to the extent of the power of insight gained by resolving each one in your study of Zen with a true master. It is the same with things of the world, but for the sake of brevity Dōgen Zenji does not go into that. Since in terms of the Buddha-dharma they are not separate, in the next chapter he takes up together the worldly and that which is beyond the world.

In order to understand the nature of the myriad dharmas, in addition to seeing the directions and circle, we should know that the mountains and oceans have whole worlds of innumerable wondrous features. We should understand that it is not only our distant surroundings that are like this, but even what is right here, even a single drop of water.

14

❧ ❧

THIS has the purpose of summarizing the previous section. In *Shōbōgenzō Naippō* in the *Collected Commentaries* it says, "As for wondrous features of oceans, the *Sutra of the Buddha's Discourse on the Eight Wondrous Features of the Ocean* explains them in detail; as for wondrous features of mountains, the forty-fourth chapter of the *Great Commentary on the Hua-Yen Sutra* takes up the wondrous features of the ten mountain kings." So, perhaps Dōgen Zenji also is indirectly extolling the spirit of those scriptures.

The expression "in order to understand the nature of the myriad dharmas" has an exquisite taste, and if I explain it I'm afraid that flavor will be lost.[102] Since it is not a particularly difficult expression to understand, I will let you get a taste of its flavor by yourself.

Taking the ocean and mountains as an example of the myriad dharmas, although the ocean looks round and the mountains look high (speaking in terms of the meaning without getting too hung up on the word *directions*), those of course are not all the wondrous features of the ocean and mountains. The ocean and mountains are endowed with innumerable wondrous features. That is not just from the perspective of scientific research. Rather, we should say that we are speaking mainly from the perspective of religion, or, more precisely, from the perspective of the penetrating examination done in the practice of the Buddha way. Accordingly, while the wondrous features of oceans and mountains are one example, as a metaphor this also points to the nature of the Buddha way. So then with that in mind try to get the flavor of the expression "we should know that the mountains and oceans have whole worlds."

Now great scientists understand quite clearly that that which can be known by the human mind is nothing more than an infinitesimal fraction of the actual universe. Therefore such things as vast boundless worlds and incalculably numerous conditions that are discussed in the scriptures are not denied by great scientists. It is scientific to say you don't understand those things that you don't understand. To rashly deny those things that you don't understand is unscientific. That kind of person is what I call a second-rate scientist. Concerning such things as matters of the spiritual world and supernormal powers as well, they simply conclude that such things are superstitions.

So naturally then, isn't it unscientific to affirm things you don't understand? Of course it is. We should never affirm that which we don't understand. However, this writer is a disciple of the Buddha, so of course I have faith in the teachings of the buddhas and ancestors. Therefore, if something is affirmed by the buddhas and ancestors and I do not understand it, I simply accept it on trust. But I would never go so far as to demand that others believe it.

Nevertheless, again and again I come across people who

profess to be disciples of the Buddha and yet don't believe in the teachings of the Buddha but just sweepingly conclude that everything that can't be proven scientifically is superstition. In the case of something that has been scientifically proven to be nonexistent, it is more excusable (though there may be a mistake), but in the case of something that cannot be scientifically proven either existent or nonexistent, I cannot at all understand how a disciple would deny its existence in spite of the fact that the buddhas teach it. So, I don't think Dōgen Zenji's phrase "we should know there are worlds" is such a simple one. Naturally you should understand that your current conditions are a result of past karma and know about the workings of samsara in the three realms and six destinies.[103]

"We should understand that it is not only our distant surroundings that are like this, but even what is right here, even a single drop of water." Concerning ourselves with "the nature of the myriad dharmas" or "there are worlds," we ignorant people forget about ourselves and randomly spend all our time looking outward. So don't think that Dōgen Zenji is talking about some other place. Pay attention to the place where you are standing. Pay attention to yourselves. Don't only look into the distance at the great ocean. There is no great ocean apart from a single drop of water. Awaken to the fact that our every step, every move, every thought is endowed with immeasurable wondrous features. In our every action we inhale and exhale the whole universe. This is what Dōgen Zenji is fervently urging us to realize.

When fish swim in the water, no matter how much they
swim the water does not come to an end. When birds fly in
the sky, no matter how much they fly, the sky does not
come to an end.[104] *However, though fish and birds have*
never been apart from the water and the air, when the need
is great the function is great; when the need is small the
function is small. Likewise, it is not that at every moment
they are not acting fully, not that they do not turn and
move freely everywhere, but if a bird leaves the air, imme-
diately it dies; if a fish leaves the water, immediately it dies.
We should realize that because of water there is life. We
should realize that because of air there is life. Because there
are birds there is life; because there are fish there is life. Life
is the bird and life is the fish. Besides this we could proceed
further. It is just the same with practice and enlightenment
and the lives of people.

USING fish and water and birds and the sky as metaphors, this section teaches us about the reality of
our practice of the Buddha way, the manifestation
of absolute reality (*genjōkōan*).

No matter how much a fish swims around in the great
ocean, there is no limit to the ocean. No matter how much a
bird flies around in the sky, there is no limit to the sky.

In the same way, whether we are aware of it or not,
throughout the twenty-four hours of the day we are always
swimming around in the great ocean of the Buddha-dharma,

flying around the great sky of the Buddha way. Though we gradually enter more and more deeply into the great ocean of the Buddha-dharma, there is no limit. The great sky of the Buddha way is vast and boundless, and no matter how much you practice, you can never exhaust that practice.

There has never been an instance of fish going out of the water or birds leaving the air. In the same way, since beginningless time we have never once been apart from the Buddha-dharma. Though we may create bad karma and fall into the pits of hell, or cultivate goodness and be reborn as heavenly beings or humans, we never depart from the dharma-nature samadhi, buddha-nature samadhi.[105] Since the whole universe is nothing but the Buddha way itself, naturally there is no entering or leaving.

Nevertheless, a whale swims around as if he owns the whole ocean and makes use of the ocean's water in a large way, while a shrimp or a small fish makes use of only a small bit of the ocean. This is the meaning of "when the need is great the function is great; when the need is small, the function is small." This too is accommodated language. In the fifth case of the *Blue Cliff Record*, Hsüeh-feng teaches the assembly saying, "Pick up the whole world between your fingers as if it were the size of a grain of millet."[106] Discrimination of big and small is part of the ordinary consciousness of deluded people, but it doesn't hold good in the realm of the original self. What big and small can there be in the world of the absolute? Even if you understand intellectually that the largest is identical with the smallest, when the reality of that is thrust before you—the whole world as a grain of millet—you're at a loss. That's proof that it's just a picture of the absolute and that the reality of it hasn't been grasped. Though Dōgen Zenji also speaks of large and small, naturally he is not in the realm of large and small.

He shows this, saying, "Likewise, it is not that at every moment they are not acting fully, not that they do not turn and move freely everywhere."

Fish and birds are discussed here as a metaphor for the naturalness of the everyday life of practitioners of the Buddha way, not to give a biological explanation of the habits of birds and fish. So, what we aim for in our practice of the Buddha way is to become "when all dharmas are the Buddha-dharma," to become "when the myriad dharmas all are without self," and further, to go "beyond abundance and scarcity." When we are always open to and function as absolute manifest reality, our going, our staying, our sitting, and our lying down, our response in every situation is the great life of the universe, the absolute life. That is called acting fully at every moment, and also turning and moving (the whole universe) freely everywhere.

"If a bird leaves the air, immediately it dies; if a fish leaves the water, immediately it dies." This expression doesn't need explanation. It merely clarifies the fact that there is no life outside the Buddha-dharma. "We should realize that because of water there is life. We should realize that because of air there is life. Because there are birds there is life; because there are fish, there is life. Life is the bird and life is the fish."

Anyone can understand that water means life to a fish and air means life to a bird. That's what is called thought. That's speaking as if we consider the fish and the water or the bird and the air to be two separate things, but in fact they are not. If we separate them, the fish and the bird are dead. The world of the oneness of the fish and the water, the nonduality of the bird and the air, the unity of man and his environment, is expressed as "because there are birds there is life," and as "life is the fish." There is no need to attach theories to it. If you call it life, then you've said everything with that one word. You may understand the meaning of the unity of man and his environment intellectually, but if you haven't clearly grasped the fact of the unity of man and his environment, when you hear "because there are birds there is life," or "life is the fish," you will not be satisfied without some sort of explanation.

"Besides this we could proceed further. It is just the same with practice and enlightenment and the lives of people." Above, where it says water is life, air is life, the bird is life, the fish is life—or rather, "life is the bird, life is the fish"—one meaning of *life* is the nonduality of man and his environment. However, we can't just experience that once and be satisfied with that. From the top of a hundred-foot pole we have to take one more step, a hundred more steps, advancing again and again. Piling practice and enlightenment upon practice and enlightenment, we must always be drawn further along by the practice based on enlightenment. Our true lives, which we call Buddha-nature, in other words life itself, is always like this. Reaching buddhahood, to say nothing of the place of nonregression in our practice, is the natural functioning of our essential self. All the buddhas of the past, present, and future are living examples of that. If one does not have the religious capacity to at least believe in and understand the existence of buddhas and bodhisattvas throughout space and time, [107] he'll have a very hard time accepting Dōgen Zenji's *Shōbōgenzō*. That's why it is said to be beyond the power of those who are simply philosophers.

So, if there were a bird or a fish that wanted to go through **16**
the sky or the water only after thoroughly investigating its
limits, he would not attain his way nor find his place in the
water or in the sky. If one attains this place, these daily
activities manifest absolute reality. If one attains this Way,
these daily activities are manifest absolute reality. This
Way, this place, is neither large nor small, neither self nor
other, has neither existed previously nor is just now mani-
festing, and thus it is just as it is.

SINCE Dōgen Zenji's writings are so truly refined, you must get a sincere taste of each word and phrase along with its context and then discern the boundless spirit behind it.

A bird or fish that wants to go through the sky or water only after it has thoroughly investigated its limits does not, of course, exist. However, people are always apt to be chasing after knowledge while taking actual practice lightly. Even from this *Shōbōgenzō* most people are only seeking intellectual understanding. Those who throw themselves into the actual practice of the *Shōbōgenzō* are few. Actual practice of the *Shōbō-genzō* means actual practice of the Buddha way. Of course the Buddha way also includes intoning the names of the buddhas and the titles of the sutras, reading the sutras, bowing, and so on, but the essential points of the actual practice of the Buddha way are the three studies: moral foundations, concentration, and wisdom, and within those zazen is the heart of the actual practice of the Buddha way. Therefore, the genuine practice of the *Shōbōgenzō* is the samadhi of zazen.

If we want to thoroughly penetrate the teachings and only then take up the actual practice of zazen, we'll be waiting forever. Dōgen Zenji expresses this metaphorically, saying the fish, or the bird, will "not attain his way nor find his place in the water or in the sky."

What does this "way" mean? Of course literally it refers to the path the fish should swim and the path the bird should fly, but it goes without saying that it refers to the correct path for the one who seeks the Way. "Place" on the surface has the sense of the place where the birds and fish can live peacefully, but it also goes without saying that this is the "place" where the true person of the Way establishes his life upon the peace of mind of resting in the original self. Therefore, if upon reading the opening passage of *Bendōwa* ("On Practicing the Way"), which is the first volume of the *Shōbōgenzō*,[108] one does not immediately enter the true gate of sitting upright in zazen, practicing the practice of the buddhas in order to truly realize supreme perfect enlightenment, she's not on the right track. This passage reads:

> All Buddha Tathagatas directly transmit the wondrous dharma and have the ultimate, unfabricated, subtle means for realizing supreme, perfect enlightenment. This is transmitted only from buddha to buddha without distortion because *jijūyū* samadhi[109] is its standard. In order to enjoy this samadhi, sitting upright in zazen is the true gate.

One may put aside the actual practice of zazen, and simply taking *Shōbōgenzō* as an object of philosophical study, earn a living as a scholar, but he shouldn't expect to obtain the true thread of the Buddha way or the place of the certitude of establishing one's life on the peace of mind of resting in the original self. If that's all a person wants, he is free to do as he pleases. But, like a person who climbs a mountain of jewels, just looks around, and vainly returns without having picked up any jewels, it is truly regrettable.

Next is "if one attains this place, these daily activities manifest absolute reality. If one attains this Way, these daily activities are manifest absolute reality." This "place" is the place of establishing one's life on the peace of mind of resting in the original self, in order words, the place of great liberation. This "way" is the thread of the Buddha way, in other words Right View, the view of the Buddha. For any person, no matter who it is, who opens up Right View and is able to live the life of great liberation, his everyday life will become manifest absolute reality (*genjōkōan*), or rather, is manifest absolute reality itself.

Next is "this Way, this place, is neither large nor small, neither self nor other, has neither existed previously nor is just now manifesting, and thus it is just as it is." What does that mean?

The Buddha way, which is also called Right View or the way of great liberation, cannot be measured in terms of large and small. Conventionally this is expressed as "in greatness it is boundless. In smallness it enters where there is no space."[110] To put it concretely, the Buddha way is spacious enough to envelop the whole universe, and yet it is fully encompassed in electrons and elementary particles. It cannot be divided up into self and other. If you say "self," the whole thing is self. If you say "other," the whole thing is other. Dividing things up between self and other is the deluded dream of the unenlightened. There is no self and other in the realm of true reality.

Dōgen Zenji calls this both "completely self" and "completely other."

Further examining the Buddha way, which we are calling absolute manifest reality, in terms of time, it "has neither existed previously nor is just now manifesting." This is not some vague thing; it is a clear, precise actuality. Since the Buddha way is the fundamental original endowment of every person, it is not something that is newly manifesting now. And yet since everyone has ignored this original endowment and thus failed to notice it, it's no good to just leave the situation as it is. This is what Dōgen Zenji is expressing when he says it "has neither existed previously nor is just now manifesting." To say it in other words, although the Buddha way is every person's original endowment, it must be realized. "It is just as it is" is a concluding phrase that ties together everything from "this Way, this place." It has the sense of thrusting forth the dharma of suchness, extolling the fact that at all times and everywhere, manifest absolute reality—that is, the Buddha way—"is just as it is."

17

Therefore, for a person who practices and realizes the Buddha way, to attain one dharma is to penetrate one dharma; to encounter one activity is to practice one activity.

⚘ ⚘

"THEREFORE" connects this to the previous section, and the understanding of the practitioner who practices and realizes the Buddha way is summed up most concisely by "to attain one dharma is to penetrate one dharma; to encounter one activity is to practice one activity." "Therefore" would perhaps be clearer if we said, "Since it is like this."

Since the Buddha way is vast and boundless, it is important to carefully examine the teachings one by one, just as we crush grains of rice one by one to make rice paste. It is extremely mistaken to think that after you understand the whole Buddha-dharma you'll put it into practice. When you understand one inch of the Buddha way, that's how much you put into practice, and when you understand one foot of the Buddha way, that's how much you put into practice. This is the fundamental style of the practice of the Buddha way.

Further, those who want to practice and actualize the Buddha way shouldn't try to know about everything or be a jack of all trades. The Buddha way is not something that can easily be attained while you busy yourself with those other things. Rather, the Buddha way can only be attained after pouring your entire life force into it.

The expression "to attain one dharma is to penetrate one

dharma; to encounter one activity is to practice one activity" has various other implications. First off, when we look at *Shōbō-genzō Zuimonki* and *Shōbōgenzō Bendōwa* we find that the one dharma and one practice in this passage refer to zazen. In our dharma lineage we strongly urge people to attain the one dharma of zazen, which is the true entrance into the Buddha way, and to penetrate the one dharma of zazen; to encounter the one practice of zazen and to practice the one practice of zazen. It goes without saying that this passage also has the sense that we don't have the time to be looking around at other dharmas and other practices or to be spending our months and years in philosophical speculation.

Well, that is what it looks like from the standpoint of practice and enlightenment. Now let's take a look at it from the standpoint of the original self. Inherently speaking, "to attain one dharma is to penetrate one dharma; to encounter one activity is to practice one activity." How else could it be? In attaining one dharma, however that may come about, we have definitely penetrated that one dharma. If we have not penetrated that one dharma, we haven't attained it. Of course, right from the start, "to attain one dharma is to penetrate one dharma." It's the same with "to encounter one activity is to practice one activity." If we meet with one activity there is nothing else we can do besides practice it. When we drink tea and eat rice, we are only drinking tea and eating rice. When we defecate and urinate, we're simply defecating and urinating. For anyone, at anytime, in any place, it's always one-practice samadhi. You may say, "Yes, but can't you sit at the table smoking a cigarette, reading the newspaper, and listening to the radio at the same time?" Of course you can do that, but when you're doing several things at the same time, all of them are halfhearted. Now think about when you are attentively reading an important book. At such a time your whole body becomes your eye. Even if you're smoking you don't notice it; you don't notice that you're sitting at the table either. Even when we appear to be paying attention to several things at once, or to be doing several things at the same time, in fact they are alternating at an awesome speed, so at any one moment it is, without a doubt, one-practice samadhi. Whether we know it or not, that's the fact.

18

Since in this is the place, and since the Way pervades everywhere, the reason that the limit of what is knowable cannot be known is that this knowledge arises and is penetrated simultaneously with the complete accomplishment of the Buddha-dharma. One should certainly not think that, attaining this place, it necessarily becomes his own perception, nor that it is a matter of knowledge. Even though complete realization is immediately manifest, it is not always seen as one's intimate being, and why need it be?

THIS chapter is full of difficult expressions, especially "the reason that the limit of what is knowable cannot be known." This has been interpreted in two ways: "we cannot know it" or "we cannot know it clearly." Since this is only a matter of degree, I think that either way of understanding it is acceptable.

Next is, "arises and is penetrated simultaneously," which means nondual, unified. "Complete accomplishment of the Buddha-dharma" is something like the culmination of the Buddha-dharma or the last word and signifies the true Buddha-dharma.

Let's examine the meaning of "in this is the place" and "the Way pervades everywhere." "In this is the place" means that at the time of one-practice *samadhi*, therein is the "place" of peaceful abiding,[111] the place of great liberation. "The Way pervades everywhere" indicates that that person is pervaded with the boundless spirit of the Buddha way and accordingly, through that person the Buddha way pervades everywhere. In other words, the boundless spirit of the Buddha way is freely and unobstructedly manifested and vividly expressed. Since that's the case, if you ask whether we can know its limits, that is, the whole of it, there is no way we can know it fully. The reason for that is that our one-activity *samadhi* is the complete accomplishment of the Buddha-dharma and is the true Buddha-dharma itself. So, just as the eye is not able to see itself, in the place where "to attain one dharma is to penetrate one dharma," in the place where "to encounter one activity is to practice one activity," the fact that the true Buddha-dharma is manifesting does not arise into our consciousness.

This fact is further clarified by the next line. "One should certainly not think that, attaining this place, it necessarily becomes his own perception, nor that it is a matter of knowledge." That means that when we attain one dharma and penetrate one dharma, meet with one activity and practice that one activity, we are actualizing the Buddha way beautifully. And yet don't think that it becomes one's own knowledge and view, or that it is something understood by the self.

"Even though complete realization is immediately manifest, it is not always seen as one's intimate being, and why need it be?" Here, "complete realization" means the same thing as "attaining this place."

It may be rather lengthy, but if we express Dōgen Zenji's words in modern language it is something like this: "In the place where attaining one dharma is penetrating that one dharma and encountering one activity is practicing that one activity, complete enlightenment, in other words, the culmination of the realization of the Buddha-dharma, is immediately actualized, or accomplished, but since it is one's intimate existence, that is, one's very self, it will not necessarily rise up into one's consciousness or be known to others. At times it may manifest but that does not necessarily have to be the case all the time."

19

As Zen master Pao-ch's of Mount Ma-ku¹¹² was fanning himself, a monk came and said, "The nature of wind is permanently abiding and there is no place it does not reach. Why, master, do you still use a fan?" The master said, "You only know that the nature of wind is permanently abiding, but you do not yet know the true meaning of 'there is no place it does not reach.'" The monk said, "What is the true meaning of 'there is no place it does not reach'?" The master just fanned himself. The monk bowed deeply.

FINALLY, we have come to the last part, in which Dōgen ties things together. In other words the dialogue about the nature of the wind permanently abiding summarizes the boundless spirit of the whole *Genjōkōan*. It's just as the opening passage of the text tells us: Realize that "all dharmas are the Buddha-dharma" and establish everything; thoroughly penetrate that "the myriad dharmas all are without self" and sweep away everything; further, go beyond abundance and scarcity, setting up and clearing away, and return to the original form where "flowers fall amid our longing and weeds spring up amid our antipathy." That's *genjōkōan*! This spirit is summed up and expressed with this dialogue on the nature of the wind permanently abiding.

Zen master Pao-ch'e of Mount Ma-ku was a dharma heir of Ma-tsu Tao-i and was a clear-eyed teacher. That's why Dōgen Zenji quotes this dialogue. "The nature of the wind is permanently abiding and there is no place it does not reach.

Why, master, do you still use a fan?" This manner of inquiring
is called a borrowed question. Borrowing the metaphor of the
wind, it asks about the essential meaning of the Buddha-
dharma. In other words, the spirit of the question is, "since
sentient beings are originally buddhas, why are practice and
realization necessary?" This is the essential point of the Buddha way and the heart of the *Genjōkōan*. The master said,
"You only know that the nature of wind is permanently abiding, but you do not yet know the true meaning of 'there is
no place it does not reach.' " Since the monk came with a
metaphorical question, the master used the same metaphor to
respond. In terms of the wind, with the exception of those
who love to argue, such a thing should be easily understood
without asking about it. So then, the important thing is to get
a taste of the spirit of his answer. In other words, he issues an
important caution, telling the monk, "You fancy that you have
grasped the meaning of the statements 'all sentient beings are
originally buddhas' or 'all sentient beings have the buddha-
nature,' but you have not yet recognized the fact that you must
realize it yourself. You haven't realized it." The monk respectfully inquires, "What is the true meaning of 'there is no place
it does not reach'?" Here again, you can't just look at the
literal meaning of the words. Beneath it is his real question,
"What is this buddha-nature with which we are originally endowed?" At that point the master remains silent and shows
him, using his fan. With this he exposes his buddha-nature
and thrusts it forth. He thrusts forth *muji*; he unsparingly reveals his original face.

"The monk bowed deeply." Whether he suddenly had a
great realization or not would probably have been clear to
Master Pao-ch'e, but we cannot tell from this record alone.

The true experience of the Buddha-dharma and its living way of correct transmission are like this. To say, "If the nature of wind is permanently abiding we need not use a fan; even when we don't use a fan there should still be wind," is to know neither the meaning of permanently abiding nor the nature of wind.

20

🌱 🌱

🌱

Because the nature of wind is permanently abiding, the wind of the house of the buddhas makes manifest the earth as pure gold and turns the long river into sweet cream.[113]

HERE Dōgen Zenji comments on the dialogue about the nature of the wind permanently abiding and ties together the whole of the *Genjōkōan*. The Buddha-dharma is entirely something to be actually realized and personally experienced. There is truly nothing more deplorable than the fact that there are many people who, though they yap on and on about "personal experience" verbally and in writing, are utterly without personal experience of realization. When we speak of the personal experience of realizing the Buddha way, actually practicing zazen and having a sudden great enlightenment is the heart of the matter. Meticulously maintaining one's practice is the light emitted by that personal experience of realization. Of course the Buddha-dharma is something we are all originally endowed with, so meticulously maintaining one's practice is nothing other than the natural manifestation of the Buddha-dharma. But that is merely "the nature of wind is permanently abiding." Without the personal experience of sudden great enlightenment, "there is no place it does not reach" is not manifest. If that is not manifest, it's not the living *Shōbōgenzō* (treasury of the true dharma eye). This is what is meant by the true experience of the (correctly transmitted) Buddha-dharma, and the correctly transmitted living way (of the Buddha-dharma). To say that since buddha-nature is permanently abiding we do not need enlightenment is truly not knowing buddha-nature and also knowing nothing of enlightenment.

Because buddha-nature is permanently abiding, to practice and realize that buddha-nature as "to attain one dharma is to penetrate one dharma; to encounter one activity is to practice one activity," and, by means of that practice and realization, to manifest it in our daily life, to bring it to full fruition, is the true wind of the family of the buddhas.

That's what is taught here as "makes manifest the earth as pure gold and turns the long river into sweet cream." According to Masunaga Reihō, "the earth as pure gold" appears in the *Amida Sutra*,[114] and "the long river as sweet cream" is from the *Flower Garland Sutra*.[115]

Pure gold and sweet cream are, of course, metaphorical expressions. His real intention here is to express great value. We think of this world as defiled and our surroundings as uninteresting. However, if you have a thoroughgoing great enlightenment to the permanent abiding of buddha-nature, fully ripen the whole of your everyday life to be manifest absolute reality, and make your life the Buddha way itself, this world immediately becomes the Pure Land of Eternally Quiescent Light.[116]

Your own surroundings as they are become the world of

nirvana, a cup of coarse tea becomes like sweet milk, boiled barley rice becomes like rich curds and has the flavor of sweet cream. Dōgen Zenji ties it all together, telling us that turning delusion into enlightenment, turning ignorance into holiness, departing from suffering and attaining joy in this way, is the true Buddha-dharma. This is expressed as "the earth as pure gold, the sweet cream of the long river."

TEXT OF THE
SHŌBŌGENZŌ
GENJŌKŌAN

HEN all dharmas are the Buddha-dharma, there are delusion and enlightenment, practice, birth, death, buddhas, and sentient beings. When the myriad dharmas all are without self, there is no delusion, no enlightenment, no buddhas, no sentient beings, no birth, and no death. Since originally the Buddha way goes beyond abundance and scarcity, there are birth and death, delusion and enlightenment, sentient beings and buddhas.

Yet, though it is like this, simply, flowers fall amid our longing and weeds spring up amid our antipathy.

Carrying the self forward to confirm [the existence of] the myriad dharmas is delusion. The myriad dharmas advancing and confirming [the existence] of the self is realization.

Those who have great realization about delusion are buddhas. Those who are greatly deluded within realization are sentient beings.

Further, there are people who attain realization upon realization and people who are deluded within delusion.

When Buddhas are truly buddhas they do not need to be aware of being buddhas. However, they are actualized buddhas and further actualize buddhahood.

In mustering the whole body and mind and seeing forms, in mustering the whole body and mind and hearing sounds, they are intimately perceived; but it is not like the reflection in a mirror, nor like the moon in the water. When one side is realized the other side is dark.

To study the Buddha way is to study oneself. To study oneself is to forget oneself. To forget oneself is to be enlightened by the myriad dharmas. To be enlightened by the myriad dharmas is to bring about the dropping away of body and mind of both oneself and others. The traces of enlightenment come to an end, and this traceless enlightenment is continued endlessly.

✣

When a person starts to search out the dharma, he separates himself far from the dharma. When the dharma has already been rightly transmitted in oneself, just then one is one's original self.

✣

If a person, when he is riding along in a boat, looks around and sees the shore, he mistakenly thinks that the bank is moving. But if he looks directly at the boat, he discovers that it is the boat that is moving along. Likewise, with confused thoughts about body and mind, holding to discrimination of the myriad dharmas, one mistakenly thinks his own mind and nature are permanent. If, intimately engaged in daily activities, one returns to right here, the principle that the myriad dharmas have no self is clear.

✣

Firewood becomes ash. It does not turn into firewood again. But we should not hold to the view that the ash is after and the firewood is before. Know that firewood abides in its dharma position as firewood and has its past and future. Though it has its past and future, it cuts off past and future. Ash is in its dharma position as ash and has its past and future. Just as this firewood, after it has become ash, does not turn into firewood again, so a person, after death, does not take rebirth. Therefore, we do not say that life becomes death. This is the established way of the Buddha-dharma. For this reason it is called unborn. Death does not become life. This is the established buddha-turning of the dharma wheel. For this reason it is called undying. Life is its own time. Death is its own time. For example, it is like winter and spring. We don't think that winter becomes spring. We don't say that spring becomes summer.

⚘

A person getting enlightened is like the moon reflecting in the water. The moon does not get wet, the water is not disturbed. Though it is a great expanse of light, it reflects in a little bit of water; the whole moon and the whole sky reflect even in the dew on the grass; they reflect even in a single drop of water. Enlightenment not disturbing the person is like the moon not piercing the water. A person not obstructing enlightenment is like the dewdrop not obstructing the heavens. The depth is the measure of the height. As for the length or brevity of the time [of the reflection], one ought to examine whether the water is large or small and discern whether the sky and moon are wide or narrow.

⚘

If the dharma has not yet fully come into one's body and mind, one thinks it is already sufficient. On the other hand, if the dharma fills one's body and mind, there is a sense of insufficiency. It is like going out in a boat in the middle of an ocean with no mountains. Looking in the four directions one only sees a circle; no distinguishing forms are seen. Nevertheless, this great ocean is neither a circle nor has directions. The wondrous features of this ocean that remain beyond our vision are inexhaustible. It is like a palace; it is like a jeweled necklace. It is just that, as far as my vision reaches for the time being, it appears to be a circle. The myriad dharmas are also

just like that. Though they include all forms within and beyond the dusty world, clear seeing and understanding only
reach as far as the power of our penetrating insight.

⚜

In order to understand the nature of the myriad dharmas, in
addition to seeing the directions and circle, we should know
that the mountains and oceans have whole worlds of innumerable wondrous features. We should understand that it is not
only our distant surroundings that are like this, but even what
is right here, even a single drop of water.

⚜

When fish swim in the water, no matter how much they swim
the water does not come to an end. When birds fly in the sky,
no matter how much they fly, the sky does not come to an
end. However, though fish and birds have never been apart
from the water and the air, when the need is great the function
is great; when the need is small the function is small. Likewise,
it is not that at every moment they are not acting fully, not
that they do not turn and move freely everywhere, but if a bird
leaves the air, immediately it dies; if a fish leaves the water,
immediately it dies. We should realize that because of water
there is life. We should realize that because of air there is life.
Because there are birds there is life; because there are fish
there is life. Life is the bird and life is the fish. Besides this we
could proceed further. It is just the same with practice and
enlightenment and the lives of people.

⚜

So, if there were a bird or fish that wanted to go through the
sky or the water only after thoroughly investigating its limits,

he would not attain his way nor find his place in the water or in the sky. If one attains this place, these daily activities manifest absolute reality. If one attains this Way, these daily activities are manifest absolute reality. This Way, this place, is neither large nor small, neither self nor other, has neither existed previously nor is just now manifesting, and thus it is just as it is.

✧

Therefore, for a person who practices and realizes the Buddha way, to attain one dharma is to penetrate one dharma; to encounter one activity is to practice one activity.

✧

Since in this is the place, and since the Way pervades everywhere, the reason that the limit of what is knowable ca₊₊not be known is that this knowledge arises and is penetrated simultaneously with the complete accomplishment of the Buddha-dharma. One should certainly not think that, attaining this place, it necessarily becomes his own perception, nor that it is a matter of knowledge. Even though complete realization is immediately manifest, it is not always seen as one's intimate being, and why need it be?

✧

As Zen master Pao-ch'e of Mount Ma-ku was fanning himself, a monk came and said, "The nature of wind is permanently abiding and there is no place it does not reach. Why, master, do you still use a fan?" The master said, "You only know that the nature of wind is permanently abiding, but you do not yet know the true meaning of 'there is no place it does not reach.' " The monk said, "What is the true meaning of 'there

is no place it does not reach'?" The master just fanned himself. The monk bowed deeply.

The true experience of the Buddha-dharma and its living way
of correct transmission are like this. To say, "If the nature of
wind is permanently abiding we need not use a fan; even when
we don't use a fan there should still be wind," is to know
neither the meaning of permanently abiding nor the nature of
wind.

Because the nature of wind is permanently abiding, the wind
of the house of the buddhas makes manifest the earth as pure
gold and turns the long river into sweet cream.

NOTES

Translator's Introduction

1. Hakuyu Taizan Maezumi, *The Way of Everyday Life* (Los Angeles: Center Publications, 1978).
2. This section about Yasutani's birth and early life is based on his "My Childhood," translated by Taizan Maezumi, *ZCLA Journal* 3, nos. 3, 4 (1973). Yasutani's comment here fits very closely with the classical conception of transmigration in Buddhism.
3. Kōun Yamada, "The Stature of Yasutani Hakuun Roshi," in *Eastern Buddhist* 7, no. 2 (1974): 118.
4. This long quote and the information in the following paragraph are from Yasutani's original preface to this work, *Shōbōgenzō Sankyū: Genjōkōan* (Tokyo: Shunjusha, 1967), pp. 17–20. Yamada's "Stature" also relies on the same source, and I have consulted his translation as well.
5. *Shōbōgenzō Sankyū: Genjōkōan*, p. 108.
6. Information for this period of Yasutani's life is largely based on Yamada, "Stature." The quote is my adaptation of Yamada's translation of Yaustani's "Epilogue to *Song in Praise of the Shushōgi*"; in Kōun Yamada, "The Stature of Yasutani Hakuun Roshi," in *Eastern Buddhist* 7, no. 2 (1974): 109.
7. Based on a personal conversation with Yasutani's son, Reverend Ryōju Yasutani, July 22, 1994.
8. Personal interview with Robert Aitken, May 8, 1979.

9. The relationship between Eido and Yasutani is described in Nyogen Senzaki, et al., *Namu Dai Bosa: A Transmission of Zen Buddhism to America* (New York: Theatre Arts Books, 1976), pp. 182–88.

10. Mui Shitsu Eido, "White Cloud," *ZCLA Journal* 3, nos. 3, 4 (1973): 50–51.

11. Yamada, "Stature," 119.

12. Translation by Kazuaki Tanahashi, in *Moon in a Dewdrop* (San Francisco: North Point Press, 1985), p. 100.

13. This quote is from *Zuimonki*, talks by Dōgen recorded by his disciple Koun Ejō. This translation is taken from Takashi James Kodera, *Dogen's Formative Years in China* (Boulder, Colo.: Prajna Press, 1980), p. 59. Kodera's work discusses Dōgen's enlightenment experience in some detail. (see pp. 58–68).

14. Rick Fields, "Buddhist America"(unpublished manuscript).

15. This case is discussed in William M. Bodiford, *Sōtō Zen in Medieval Japan* (Honolulu: University of Hawaii Press, 1993), p. 150 and chap. 12, "Koan Zen."

16. Kodera, *Dogen's Formative Years*, pp. 30–31.

17. Shōhaku Okumura and Taigen Dan Leighton, *Bendōwa: Talk on Wholehearted Practice of the Way* (Kyoto: Kyoto Soto Zen Center, 1993), p. 31.

18. See Shōhaku Okumura, trans., *Shōbōgenzō-zuimonki: Sayings of Eihei Dōgen Zenji Recorded by Koun Ejō* (Kyoto: Kyoto Soto Zen Center, 1987), pp. 141–44.

19. From *Bendōwa*, in Tanahashi, *Moon in a Dewdrop*, p. 145.

20. Carl Bielefeldt offers an extended discussion of this point in his *Dōgen's Manuals of Zen Meditation* (Berkeley: University of California Press, 1988), pp. 149–60. He also traces the view of modern Soto orthodoxy—that Dōgen's Zen is exclusively *shikantaza* and is incompatible with koan Zen—to the Edo period scholar-monk Menzan Zuihō (1683–1769).

21. Dōgen, echoing the teachings of Bodhidharma, says in his *Fukan Zazengi* that those who want to practice the dharma of the ancient sages "should learn to take the backward step of

turning the light [of awareness] on itself. Then body and mind will naturally fall away, and your original face will manifest."

22. *Shōbōgenzō Sankyū: Genjōkōan*, p. 108.

23. Isshū Miura and Ruth Fuller Sasaki, *Zen Dust: The History of the Koan and Koan Study in Rinzai (Lin-chi) Zen* (New York: Harcourt, Brace and World, 1966), p. 69.

Flowers Fall

1. *Wu-men-kuan* (J: *Mumonkan*), or "Gateless Barrier," which comprises forty-eight koans with verses appended by Wu-men Hui-k'ai (1183–1260), is the most broadly known and used koan collection. This story appears in case 6. According to Zen tradition, Mahakashyapa thus became the first ancestor of Zen in India.

2. This discussion of the absolute position and relative position is based on the Five Ranks, attributed to Tung-shan Liang-chieh (J: Tōzan Ryōkai; 807–869), cofounder of the Ts'ao-tung (J: Sōtō) sect, of which Dōgen is the first Japanese patriarch. For comments on the Five Ranks by Ts'ao-shan, Tung-shan's main dharma heir, see Thomas Cleary, *Timeless Spring* (New York: Grove, 1980), pp. 51–52; for more by Tsao-shan as well as comments by the Chinese Rinzai master Fen-yang Shan-chao (947–1024) see Cleary & Cleary, *Blue Cliff Record*, pp. 637–39; and for a commentary on the Five Ranks by Hakuin see *Zen Dust*, pp. 62–72.

3. J: *Ishin denshin*, transmission of mind by mind. This phrase is attributed to Bodhidharma.

4. *Shōbōgenzō Naippō* is a commentary by Fuyō Rōran (1724–1825), published in 1791. It is based on an earlier commentary by Tenkei Denson (1648–1735), *Shōbōgenzō Benchū*, 1730. These are two of the important commentaries within the Soto tradition.

5. Quoted from *Shōbōgenzō Bendōwa*, where Dōgen comments on the realization he attained under his master T'ien-t'ung Ju-ching in China.

6. Taizan Maezumi, *Hazy Moon of Enlightenment* (Los Angeles: Center Publications, 1977), p. 153, attributes to Ch'ing-yuan Wei-hsin (J: Seigen Ishin) the following:

> For thirty years before I had penetrated Zen, when I saw mountains, they were mountains; when I saw rivers, they were rivers. Later, after I had intimately met my master and gained the entry point, when I saw mountains, they were not mountains; when I saw rivers, they were not rivers. But now that I have attained the state of essential repose, when I see mountains, they are just mountains; when I see rivers, they are just rivers.

7. This is a reference to one of the types of wisdom in a scheme of Four Wisdoms found in various schools of Buddhism: 1. The great mirror-like wisdom; 2. the wisdom of equality; 3. the wisdom of subtle observation; and 4. the perfecting-of-action wisdom. Reference to no. 3 is also made below in the text.

8. According to Zen legend, the fifth patriarch, Hung-jen (J: Gunin; 601-674), called for his disciples to write verses expressing their realization, in order to determine who would succeed him in the dharma. Shen-hsiu responded with the verse:

> The body is a Bodhi tree
> And the mind a mirror bright
> Carefully wipe them over and over
> And let no dust alight.

Hung-jen transmitted the dharma to Hui-neng (J: Enō; 638–713), an uneducated woodcutter and rice pounder, after Hui-neng composed his famous verse:

> Bodhi originally has no tree
> Nor stand of mirror bright
> Originally there is not a single thing
> So where can dust alight?

(Adapted from translation by A. F. Price and Wong Mou-lam, *The Diamond Sutra and the Sutra of Hui-neng* (Boulder: Shambhala Publications, 1969), pp. 15, 18.

9. Quoting the last line of Dōgen's *Fukan Zazengi*.
10. This refers to one's duly received body and mind according to past karma, and to the whole universe upon which they depend for their existence.
11. This is a reference to "Huang-lung's Three Barriers" in the appendix to the *Wu-men-kuan*. Huang-lung Hui-nan (J: Ōryō Enan; 1002–1069) was the founder of an important line within the Rinzai school of Zen. See Kōun Yamada, *Gateless Gate* (Tucson: University of Arizona Press, 1991), pp. 235–41.
12. Ma-tsu Tao-i (J: Baso Dōitsu; 709–788). See *Wu-men-kuan*, cases 30 and 33.
13. This incident, found in the "Skillful Means" chapter of the *Lotus Sutra*, is also referred to by Dōgen in *Bendōwa*, in the answer to question no. 3. The One Buddha Vehicle is the teaching emphasizing the absolute nature of all dharmas (constituents of existence) without distinction. In actually treading the path of the buddhas, there is only the one way of according with the absolute true nature of all things. All other teachings, which are established as temporary, expedient devices in response to the differing capacities and inclinations of sentient beings, ultimately lead to this One Buddha Vehicle. See Leon Hurvitz, *Scripture of the Lotus Blossom of the Fine Dharma* (New York: Columbia University Press, 1976), p. 29.
14. *Hsin-hsin-ming* (J: *Shinjinmei*), attributed to Seng-ts'an (J: Sōsan; d. 606), the third ancestor of Chinese Zen. The first line of this text is quoted in *Shōbōgenzō Zuimonki*. See Okumura, *Shōbōgenzō-zuimonki*, p. 195.
15. This reading of a famous line from the *Mahaparinirvana Sutra* is Dōgen's unique way of understanding this line. Previous to him the line had been read to mean "all sentient beings without exception have the buddha-nature."
16. Hsuan-sha Shih-pei (J: Gensha Shibi; 835–908), a successor of Hsüeh-feng I-ts'un (J: Seppō Gison; 822–908), was a progenitor of the Fa-yen (J: Hōgen) line of Chinese Zen.

17. Ch'ang-sha Chiang-ts'en (J: Chōsha Keijin; n.d.), a successor of Nan-ch'uan Pu-yuan (J: Nansen Fugan; 748–835; see note 69 below).
18. Chao-chou Ts'ung-shen (J: Jōshū Jūshin; 778–897), the most brilliant successor of Nan-ch'uan, is well known for numerous dialogues that have been transmitted in the form of koan. A dialogue similar to this one appears in Cleary & Cleary, *Blue Cliff Record*, case 2, pp. 10–17.
19. There are various compilations of the *Shōbōgenzō*. The seventy-five-chapter version was compiled by Dōgen himself. The larger ninety-five-chapter version, which places *Bendōwa* first, was compiled after Dōgen's death.
20. The "gate of helping by establishing differences" refers to a teacher's affirmation of relative distinctions, such as good and bad, and delusion and enlightenment, for the sake of establishing closer contact with a student and leading him along the path; in other words, it is the use of skillful means. Further on in the text, it is contrasted with the "gate of sweeping away differences."
21. For a discussion of Yasutani's relationship with Nishiari, see the introduction.
22. Various ways of referring to the absolute. The term "true form" appears in the phrase "the true form of no-form," along with the term *shōbōgenzō* in case 6 of the *Wu-men-kuan*.
23. Lin-chi I-hsüan (J: Rinzai Gigen; d. 866), founder of the Lin-chi school, is universally revered as a great Zen teacher. His very direct shouting-and-beating style was inherited from his teacher, Huang-po Hsi-yün (J: Ōbaku Kiyun; d. ca. 850). Lin-chi's four views: 1. Sometimes I snatch away the person but not the objective world; 2. sometimes I snatch away the objective world but not the person; 3. sometimes I snatch away both the person and the objective world; and 4. sometimes I snatch away neither the person nor the objective world.
24. Being utterly free from any distinction of knowing subject or knowable object.

25. Analects (Ch: *Lun-yu*) 2:17. Clearly Yasutani here is giving new interpretation to the words of Confucius and not suggesting that this is the intent of the original passage.

26. *Muji* here refers to the koan "Chao-chou's Mu," the first koan used by Yasutani and by most other Zen masters in Japan. In Kapleau's *Three Pillars of Zen* (p. 70), Yasutani says, "Because Mu is utterly impervious to logic and reason, and in addition is easy to voice, it has proven itself an exceptionally wieldy scalpel for extirpating from the deepest unconscious the malignant growth of 'I' and 'not-I' which poisons the Mind's inherent purity and impairs its fundamental wholeness."

27. Feng-hsüeh Yen-chao (J: Fuketsu Enshō; 896–973) an important master in the transmission of the Lin-chi lineage three generations after Lin-chi. The translation of this passage is taken from Cleary and Cleary, *Blue Cliff Record*, p. 347.

28. Hsüeh-tou Chang-t'ung (J: Setchō Jōtsū; n.d.) was a contemporary of Feng-hsüeh, and a disciple of Ch'ang-sha Ching-ts'en (J: Chōsha Keijin; n.d.). He is not to be mistaken for Hsüeh-tou Ch'ung-hsien (J: Setchō Jūken; 980–1052), who was a master in the fourth generation of the Yun-men school and whose verses are appended onto the cases of the *Blue Cliff Record*.

29. Since the Buddha way must be realized directly by each person, Zen teachers have traditionally been careful not to fill up students' heads with ideas and explanations. If one speaks too much, he is said to harm or decrease his virtue, as words and thought have a limiting function. We can see this principle at work in the story of the enlightenment of Hsiang-yen Chih-hsien (J: Kyōgen Chikan; n.d.). Training under Kuei-shan Ling-yu (J: Isan Reiyū; 771–853), Hsiang-yen reached a point of despair when upon asking his teacher's instruction he was told, "Even if I might show it to you, it is my word and has nothing to do with your answer." He burnt all his books and went off to live as a grave keeper. One day while sweeping, he was enlightened upon hearing

the sound of a pebble striking a bamboo. At that point he said, "The compassion of Kuei-shan is indeed greater than that of my parents. Had he taught 'it' to me when I asked him, I could never have had this great joy today" (from Zenkei Shibayama, *Zen Comments on the Mumonkan* (San Francisco: Harper and Row, 1974), pp. 54–55). Nevertheless, of all the schools of Buddhism, the writings and records of the Zen tradition are the most voluminous.

Regarding losing one's eyebrows, it is a sign of losing one's virtue by speaking too much. See Cleary and Cleary, *Blue Cliff Record*, case 8, pp. 53–58.

30. The Japanese word for delusion, *mayoi*, can also be understood as "to become lost."

31. This quote and "attaining enlightenment comes before awakening," below, are from section 3 of *Gakudō yōjinshū* (Guidelines for Studying the Way). Tanahashi (in *Moon in a Dewdrop*, p. 34) translates the passage as, "You should know that arousing practice in the midst of delusion, you attain realization before you recognize it."

32. This scheme appears in Chih-i's *Mo-ho-chih-kuan*, the basic meditation text of the T'ien-t'ai (J: Tendai) school of Buddhism. The scheme depicts the actualization of one's intrinsic Buddhahood in six stages. To briefly summarize: 1. Identity in principle, the identity of all things with the ultimate truth though it is not realized; 2. verbal identity, verbal comprehension of the teaching of the one reality of enlightenment that one has read in the sutras or heard from teachers; 3. identity of religious practice, in which one's mind starts to accord with the teachings one has learned at the previous level, and contemplation of one's thought is continuous; 4. identity of resemblance, in which contemplation progresses and wisdom that resembles the middle way is achieved; 5. identity of partial truth, entered by the power of contemplation at the previous level, in which ignorance begins to be destroyed and one perceives buddha-nature, including various stages leading up to near-buddhahood; 6. ultimate identity, in which wisdom is complete and perfect,

all defilements have been destroyed, and full buddhahood is attained. Neal Arvid Donner, "The Great Calming and Contemplation of Chih-I" (Ph.D. diss., University of British Columbia, n.d.), pp. 163–70.

33. Thomas Cleary, in *Timeless Spring*, p. 28, attributes this to Shih-t'ou Hsi-ch'ien (J: Sekitō Kisen: 700–790), an important early master who studied with the sixth patriarch, Hui-neng (J: Enō), as a youth and later transmitted the dharma from one of his two main successors, Ch'ing-yuan Hsing-ssu (J: Seigen Gyōshi). His lineage later includes Tung-shan (J: Tōzan) and Ts'ao-shan (Sōzan), founders of the Ts'ao-tung (Soto) school. Shih-t'ou is also well known as the author of the "Tsan-t'ung-chi'i" (J: Sandōkai; The Unity of Relative and Absolute). For a translation of Ts'an-t'ung-ch'i, see *Timeless Spring*, pp. 36–39.

34. Quoted from Dōgen's *Shōbōgenzō Shōji* (Birth and Death).

35. In Buddhist cosmology, Mount Sumeru is the mountain at the center of the universe.

36. Often quoted by Hakuin who attributes it to Ta-hui Tsung-kao (J: Daie Sōkō; 1089–1163), an influential Sung dynasty Zen master; see Norman Waddell, trans. "Wild Ivy: The Spiritual Autobiography of Hakuin Ekaku," Part Two. *The Eastern Buddhist*, Vol. XVI, No. 1 (Spring 1983), p. 122. Dōgen was particularly critical of Ta-hui, possibly to disabuse some of his own disciples of views they had obtained while studying with Dainichi Nōnin. Dainichi had had his realization confirmed by Ta-hui indirectly by sending a letter to him via two of his students going to China.

37. *Wu-men-kuan*, case 31.

38. *Tathagata* (J: Nyorai) is a term the Buddha used to refer to himself. Literally, it means "thus come" or "thus gone."

39. *Lotus Sutra*, chap. 16, "The Lifespan of the Tathagata." Shakyamuni Buddha in this quote clarifies the purpose behind all the various teachings he has given. See Hurvitz, *Scripture of the Lotus*, p. 244.

40. J: Nyoirin Kannon. This form of the Bodhisattva of Compassion holds the wheel of the dharma (signifying the liber-

ating teaching of the Buddha) in one hand and the jewel that grants the wishes of sentient beings in the other.

41. J: Jizō Bosatsu. This bodhisattva is entrusted with the task of saving sentient beings between the time of Shakyamuni's passing and the appearance of Maitreya, the Buddha of the Future. He vowed not to attain enlightenment until saving all other sentient beings in the six realms of existence— heavenly deities, humans, fighting spirits, animals, hungry ghosts, and hell-dwellers.

42. *Just* here translates the Japanese *shikan*. The sense of it is not "merely" doing something, but rather doing only that one thing totally.

43. See note 29 above.

44. Ling-yun Chih-ch'in (Reiun Shigon; n.d.) was a disciple of Kuei-shan Ling-yu (J: Isan Reiyū; 771–853), cofounder of the Kuei-yang (J: Igyō) line of Zen. Ling-yun attained realization upon seeing peach blossoms.

45. This is used in a talk by Po-yun Wu-liang (J: Hakuun Muryō; ca. 1425). The first character is the famous Zen shout, Ka! See Miura, *Zen Dust*, p. 316, n. 147.

46. According to Miura, *Zen Dust*, p. 254, this phrase first appears in the *Hua-yen Ching* (J: Kegonkyō; S: Avatamsaka Sutra).

47. From the enlightenment verses of Hsiang-yen and Ling-yun respectively, which Dōgen quotes in his *Shōbōgenzō Keiseisanshiki* (Sounds of Valley Streams, Forms of the Mountains). See Francis Dojun Cook, *How to Raise an Ox* (Los Angeles: Center Publications, 1978), p. 105.

48. Su Tung-p'o (J: Sotoba; 1037-1101) is generally considered the greatest poet of Sung dynasty China. Dōgen comments on Su Tung-p'o's enlightenment and quotes the verse from which this line was taken in his *Keiseisanshiki*, which also takes its name from the same verse. Cook, *Ox*, pp. 101–103.

49. *Seamless stupa* refers to a kind of egg-shaped grave marker for a monk, but obviously it is being used for its larger metaphorical meaning. The term appears in several koan

collections including the *Blue Cliff Record*, case 18 (Cleary and Cleary, pp. 115–22).

50. A line from Hsüeh-t'ou's verse in the *Blue Cliff Record*, case 40, which is cited parenthetically by Yasutani.

51. According to Kapleau, *Three Pillars of Zen*, n. 14, p. 215, this phrase originally comes from an early Chinese work and is quoted by Dōgen in the *Shōbōgenzō*.

52. This is a New Year's poem by Nakagawa Sōen Roshi (1907–1984).

53. *Mind-only* (J: *yuishin*) is a term that represents a stream of Buddhist thought that originated in the Indian Tathatagatagarbha school and in China came to be most closely associated with the Hua-yen (J: Kegon) school. By using it in parallel with *matter-only*, Yasutani is treating it in an unorthodox manner.

54. These two phrases are attributed to the sixth patriarch, Hui-neng, and appear in a koan in the *Shūmon Kattōshū*, according to Miura, *Zen Dust*, pp. 248–49, n. 33. Similar phrases are found in the *Wu-men-kuan*, case 23, and in later versions of the *Platform Sutra of the Sixth Patriarch*. The phrase *original face* is also used by Dōgen in several chapters of the *Shōbōgenzō*.

55. See note 9 above.

56. *Being one single piece* (J: *tajō ippen*), according to Hisao Inagaki, *Glossary of Zen Terms* (Kyoto: Nagata Bunshodo, 1991), p. 392, is found in Cleary and Cleary, *Blue Cliff Record*, case 6, pp. 37–45, and *Book of Serenity* (Ch: Tsungjung lu, J: Shōyōroku), case 51 (see Thomas Cleary, trans., *Book of Serenity* [New York: Lindisfarne Press, 1990]).

57. *Right mindfulness* is seventh aspect of the Buddha's Noble Eightfold Path.

58. The activities of body, speech, and mind. This and the next two sentences paraphrase a passage from Dōgen's *Bendōwa*. Cf. Tanahashi, *Moon in a Dewdrop*, p. 145; Okumura, *Bendōwa*, p. 34. Yasutani goes on to quote the passage more precisely.

59. Tanahashi, *Moon in a Dewdrop*, p. 151; Okumura, *Bendōwa*, pp. 47–48.
60. Tanahashi, *Moon in a Dewdrop*, pp. 151–52; Okumura, *Bendōwa*, p. 48.
61. *Original enlightenment* and *marvelous practice* are two phrases used in parallel in the *Bendōwa*. Based on the discussion in that text, especially the answer to question no. 7, as well as other writings of Dōgen, each one is sometimes said to represent both.
62. A reference to the teachings of Shinran (1173–1262), founder of the True Pure Land Sect (J: *Jōdo Shinshū*) of Japanese Buddhism. In contrast to the earlier Pure Land teachings, in which salvation is attained through faith in Amida Buddha, Shinran taught the unity of faith and salvation, asserting that it is not we who choose to have faith, but rather that our faith is a result of Amida's grace. For him chanting the name of Amida Buddha is not an assertion of faith, much less a means to a spiritual goal, but rather an expression of gratitude.
63. *Wu-men-kuan*, case 16, found in the commentary on the main case.
64. This phrase is attributed to Bodhidharma, the first ancestor of Zen in China, as part of the famous verse in which he delineates the basic principles of Zen:

> A special transmission outside the scriptures,
> Not founded upon words and letters,
> Directly pointing to the mind,
> Seeing one's nature and attaining buddhahood.

For more detail both on *seeing one's nature* and on this verse, see Miura, *Zen Dust*, pp. 228–30.
65. *Bendōwa*. Cf. Tanahashi, *Moon in a Dewdrop*, p. 145.
66. According to Okubo Doshu, *Dōgen zenji den no Kenkyū* (2nd ed.; Tokyo: Chikuma Shobo, 1971), p. 173, both of these phrases, which were expressed by Dōgen shortly after his return from China, are found in *Dōgen Oshō Eihei Kōroku I*.

67. This metaphor is based on a koan involving the Chinese Zen master Po Chang (J: Hyakujō; 720–814), successor of Ma-tsu and a forebear of the Rinzai line. When he was asked, "What is Buddha?" he answered, "It is like a man who seeks an ox while riding on it." The questioner pursued it, asking, "What happens when he realizes it?" "It is like a man who returns home riding on the ox." Zenkei Shibayama, *A Flower Does Not Talk* (Boston: Charles E. Tuttle, 1970), p. 95. It also suggests the "oxherding pictures" that illustrate the path of Zen. For a discussion of them, see D. T. Suzuki, *Manual of Zen Buddhism* (New York: Grove, 1987), pp. 128–44.

68. A phrase from Hakuin's *Zazen Wasan*, or Song of Zazen. See Suzuki, *Manual of Zen Buddhism*, pp. 151–52. Also Shibayama, *A Flower Does Not Talk*, pp. 65–67, and Miura, *Zen Dust*, pp. 251–53.

69. Nan-ch'üan P'u-yüan (J: Nansen Fugan; 748–835), one of the key figures in the "golden age" of Zen, was a disciple of Ma-tsu Tao-i and the teacher of Chao-chou Ts'ung-shen (J: Jōshū Jūshin; 778–897). He appears in many well-known koans. This quote is recorded in the *Tsung-jung lu* (J: Shōyōroku), case 69; see Cleary, *Book of Serenity*, p. 290. For Nan-ch'uan's biography, see Miura, *Zen Dust*, pp. 272–74, and Cleary, *Blue Cliff Record*, pp. 598–600.

70. This question is part of a conversation that had a strong impact on Dōgen immediately upon his arrival in China. It is recounted in detail in *Tenzo kyōkun*; see Dogen and Kōshō Uchiyama, *Refining Your Life* (New York: Weatherhill, 1983), pp. 10–11; Tanahashi, *Moon in a Dewdrop*, pp. 58–60.

71. This metaphor relates to a famous parable in the *Lotus Sutra*. See Hurvitz, *Scripture of the Lotus*, chap. 4, "Belief and Understanding."

72. Regarding Shih-t'ou Hsi-ch'ien, see note 33 above. This quote can be found in *Transmission of the Lamp*, section 14. Diligence (S: *virya*) and concentration (S: *samadhi*) are two of the *paramitas*, virtues to be perfected in the course of

Buddhist training. Shih-t'ou here echoes a famous statement from the "Skillful Means" chapter of the *Lotus Sutra*
and also conveys the main thrust of the teaching of the sixth
patriarch. For a more detailed biography, see Miura, *Zen
Dust*, pp. 300–302.

73. This and the following quote are from *Bendōwa*; see Okumura, *Bendōwa*, p. 30; Tanahashi, *Moon in a Dewdrop*, p.
143.

74. See note 66 above.

75. The five *skandas,* heaps or aggregates, are a teaching of the
Buddha that analyzes human experience into form, feeling,
perception (including thought), volition, and consciousness. The point of the teaching is to observe one's own
experience in such a way as to recognize that there is no
abiding, permanent self that is the subject of experience.

76. I could not locate this quote, but there is a similar one in
Dōgen's *Shisho* (Document of Succession): "When chrysanthemums inherit from chrysanthemums and a pine gives
the seal of realization to a pine, the preceding chrysanthemum is one with the following chrysanthemum, and the
preceding pine is one with the following pine." Translation
from Tanahashi, *Moon in a Dewdrop*, p. 187.

77. A Mahayana sutra translated into Chinese by Buddhatara
in 693. For a translation see Lu K'uan Yü, *Ch'an and Zen
Teaching*, vol. 3 (York Beach, Me.: Samuel Weiser, 1993).

78. See note 75 above.

79. *Principle*, here, translates the Japanese *dōri*, the second
character of which is *ri*, often translated in a Buddhist context as principle, absolute, noumenon, ultimate reality. One
important aspect of the teaching of Hua-yen Buddhism,
which historically was closely tied with Zen, is the mutual
interpenetration of *ri* with *ji*, things or phenomenal existence. It is also an important principle in the Mahayana
treatise *The Awakening of Faith* (translated into Chinese by
Paramartha in 550), where the metaphor of waves and
water is used. For an English translation, see Yoshito S.

Hakeda, *The Awakening of Faith* (New York: Columbia University Press, 1967).

80. In the Buddhist psychological canon, a *kshana* is the shortest distinguishable period of time, sometimes referred to as a mind moment. Here Yasutani is referring to the number of *kshana* in one day. There are a variety of ways of calculating them.

81. This poem is full of word plays, and it could also be read:

> The body of existence
> And nonexistence
> Are both this one body,
> In emptiness,
> There are not two tastes.

82. The ideogram used here can mean either birth or life, or probably a more accurate way to think about it in this case, both. In English it is necessary to give primacy to one or the other depending on the context.

83. The four phrases mentioned are central to the philosophy of Nāgārjuna, whose Mādhyamika, or middle way, teaching is an important basis for the development of Mahayana Buddhism. The *Mādhyamika Shastra*, attributed to Nāgārjuna, was translated into Chinese at the beginning of the fifth century. This work, like the *Mūlamādhyamika Kārikā* and other works by Nāgārjuna, systematically demonstrates the untenability of any view one might hold regarding the nature of existence, with the aim of springing the reader into the recognition of the inconceivable. References to these four phrases, often taken to represent all categorization and discrimination, are found frequently in Zen literature. For more on the Mādhyamika, see Richard Robinson, *Early Mādhyamika in India and China* (Delhi: Motilal Banarsidass, 1976), which includes what might be considered proto-Zen writings.

84. *The Song of the Enlightened Way* was written by Yung-chia Hsüan-chüeh (J: Yōka Genkaku: d. 713), better known as Yung-chia Ta-shih (J: Yōka Daishi). Originally a student of

T'ien-t'ai Buddhism, he went to study with the sixth ancestor and attained enlightenment. He expressed his understanding in this long poem, which is generally considered to be one of the few reliable writings of the very early period of Chinese Zen. For translations, see Suzuki, *Manual of Zen Buddhism*, pp. 89–103; Lu, *Chan and Zen Teachings*, vol. 3, 116–45. For a biography see Chang Chung-yuan, *Original Teachings of Ch'an Buddhism* (New York: Random House, 1969), pp. 27–34.

85. Dharma position (J: *hō-i*) originally comes from the *Lotus Sutra*, where it indicates that the truth pointed to by the Buddha's teaching is a stable and abiding support. However, it was read by Chih-i, the founder of the T'ien-t'ai school to refer to the suchness of all things, absolute as they are. This then became the traditional understanding of the term in East Asia, and is the sense in which Dōgen uses it here.

86. Masamune Okazaki was a swordmaker in the Kamakura period (1185–1392) who studied the secret techniques of the ancient swordmakers and produced incomparable weapons.

87. *Shushōgi* is a text comprising various excerpts from Dōgen's writings that was put together around 1888. It is used as a congregational text by the Soto sect.

88. Here Yasutani puns on the word translated as "study of principles," which is a homonym with the Japanese word for cucumber. I have abbreviated the English, but it could also read "cucumberology or eggplantology." Here he mocks the attitude of trying to grasp religious experience with logic.

89. Tao-wu Yuan-chih (J: Dōgo Enchi; 769–835) appears in a famous dialogue with Shih-t'ou Hsi-ch'ien (J: Sekitō Kisen), whom he studied under (see Miura, *Zen Dust*, pp. 301–302). Later he became a dharma heir of Yüeh-shan Wei-yen (J: Yakusan Igen; 745–828), one of Shih-t'ou's two most important disciples and one of the forerunners of the

Tsao-tung (J: Sōtō) school. For Tao-wu's biography see Cleary and Cleary, *Blue Cliff Record*, pp. 619–20.

90. See note 13 above.

91. An ancient poem of unknown authorship.

92. Joy of the third Dhyana heaven: One of the four stages of *dhyana* (meditation) within the world of form, it is characterized by renunciation, right thought, right wisdom, joy, and samadhi. This joy is a contented and energetic one, in which the body and mind are completely at ease.

93. See note 62 above.

94. This passage as quoted here has a slight abridgement in the middle. Cf. Tanahashi, *Moon in a Dewdrop*, p. 37.

95. This quote, and the one below regarding self-nature, are from Hakuin's *Song of Zazen*. See note 68 above.

96. For these two quotes, see notes 59 and 73 above, respectively.

97. The same term, *jisetsu*, is used in the original, but it is translated differently to fit the context.

98. See note 36 above.

99. "Cut off the demon's head" specifically refers to the "demon" of the delusion of self, but it also has something of the sense of "having the world by the tail."

100. *Ordinary human consciousness* here refers to the state of mind of the common person, which is obscured by mistaken views and perception as well as by emotional attachments.

101. The five desires are for the objects of the five senses. The six dusts are those objects themselves—sights, sounds, smells, tastes and objects of tactile sensation—along with mental objects. Because of our dualistic grasping after these objects, our originally pure mind-nature is defiled. Thus they are called the six dusts.

102. *Nature of the myriad dharmas* here could be more literally rendered as "the wind of the house (or family) of the myriad dharmas." This phrase is paralleled in the last sentence of *Genjōkōan*, where the phrase "the wind of the house (or family) of the buddhas" appears.

103. The three realms in which sentient beings are reborn in endless rounds of suffering are 1. the realm of desire; 2. the realm of form; and 3. the formless realm. The realm of desire is that in which beings are subject to sensuous desires, especially for sex and food. It includes the beings of all the *six destinies*, the hell-dwellers, hungry ghosts, animals, *ashuras* (titans), humans, and *devas*. The realm of form is full of wondrous forms and is inhabited strictly by *devas* of a higher level than those in the realm of desire. It includes the four *dhyana*, or meditation, heavens. The formless realm is a supermaterial one where spirit alone exists. It is the place where those who have mastered the four boundless *samadhis* (of loving-kindness, compassion, joy, and equanimity) are reborn. In the larger picture, none of these places is a desirable destination, as none of them is totally free from attachment and thus all lead one to further rounds of suffering in *samsara*.

104. In this passage *sky* and *air* both translate the Japanese *sora*, according to the context.

105. In *Shōbōgenzō Hosshō* (Dharma Nature), Dōgen quotes Ma-tsu Tao-i as follows: "All sentient beings since countless eons past have never departed from dharma-nature *samadhi*. Putting on their clothes, eating and drinking, talking together, they are always within dharma-nature *samadhi*. The functioning of the mind and the senses, and every activity, is nothing but dharma-nature *samadhi*" (Terada Tōru and Mizuno Yaoko, eds., *Dōgen*, vol. 2 [Tokyo: Iwanami Shoten, 1972], p. 84).

106. For Hsüeh-feng's biography see Cleary and Cleary, *Blue Cliff Record*, p. 31 and pp. 570–72.

107. *Believe in and understand* (*shin-ge*) as it is used here by Yasutani is probably intended as the first part of a formulaic expression of the course of Buddhist practice, "believe in, understand, practice, and realize (*shin-ge-gyō-shō*)."

108. In the ninety-five chapter edition of *Shōbōgenzō*, compiled after Dōgen's death, the *Bendōwa* chapter is placed first.

For this passage see Tanahashi, *Moon in a Dewdrop*, p. 143; Okumura, *Bendōwa*, pp. 29–30.

109. *Jijūyū samadhi* is the *samadhi* of receiving and using one's true self freely. Tanahashi (*Moon in a Dewdrop*, p. 328) renders it as *self-fulfilling samadhi*. Okumura (*Bendōwa*, p. 25) characterizes it as, "Our life is pervading the whole universe, and yet my life is just myself."

110. Two lines from Tung-shan's *Jewel Mirror Samadhi*, an important text in the Soto sect, although Dōgen never refers to it in his writings. For a translation of the text see Cleary, *Timeless Spring*, pp. 39–45.

111. *Peaceful abiding* here translates the Japanese *anjū*, which among other things is used to refer to the *samadhi* of a bodhisattva, or to one who has attained buddhahood.

112. Ma-ku-shan Pao-ch'e (J: *Maku-san Hotetsu*, n.d.), a dharma heir of Ma-tsu, was active in the eighth century. He appears in case 31 of the *Blue Cliff Record*. For biographical information on Pao-ch'e, see Cleary and Cleary, *Blue Cliff Record*, pp. 600–601.

113. *Sweet cream* here translates the Chinese *su-lao* (J: *soraku*), sometimes rendered as koumiss, a kind of fermented milk drink extolled for its health and life-giving qualities. Sweet cream is used as a translation here as it is more accessible to an English-speaking audience. Although Yasutani, below, points out other references, Dōgen, who was widely read in the Zen literature, probably was familiar with the recorded talks of Huang-lung, where we find very similar language to these last paired phrases: "changes the great earth into pure gold, and churns the long river into *soraku* (Fujiyoshi, *Zenkan Sakushin*, p. 39). Inagaki in his *Glossary of Zen Terms*, p. 30, renders *soraku* as "cream and ghee," probably having in mind the *Nirvana Sutra's* division of the Buddhist teachings into five states, each compared to a flavor developed in the process of making ghee, or clarified butter, a valued substance in India often used for ceremonial purposes. Dōgen's image may well play upon this image.

114. Known as such in Japan because of the important place of

Buddha Amitayus in this sutra. It is more properly known as the Smaller Sukhāvatīvyūha Sūtra. For a translation see Hisao Inagaki, *Three Pure Land Sutras*, (Kyoto: Nagota Bushodo, 1994).

115. *The Flower Garland Sutra* is the *Avatamsaka* (Ch: Hua-yen; J: Kegon) *Sutra*, an extremely important sutra in the development of Chinese and Japanese Buddhism. Hua-yen Buddhism in China was closely related with Zen during its early period. For a translation see Thomas Cleary, trans., *The Flower Ornament Scripture*, 3 vols. (Boston: Shambhala Publications, 1985–1987).

116. In a T'ien-t'ai (J: Tendai) classification of four buddha-lands, the Pure Land of Eternally Quiescent Light is the abode of those who have put an end to delusion and attained true wisdom; in other words, the abode of the buddha tathagatas. It also signifies the perfect identity of stillness and action.

BIBLIOGRAPHY

Anesaki Masaharu. *Religious Life of the Japanese People*. Tokyo: Kokusai Bunka Shinkokai, 1970

Ban Tetsugyū. "Dharma Words." Translated by Taizan Maezumi. *ZCLA Journal* 3, nos. 3, 4 (1973): 26–27.

Bielefeldt, Carl William. "Shōbōgenzō-sansuikyō." Master's thesis, University of California, Berkeley, 1972.

————, Carl. *Dōgen's Manuals of Zen Meditation*. Berkeley: University of California Press, 1988.

Bodiford, William M. *Sōtō Zen in Medieval Japan*. Honolulu: University of Hawaii Press, 1993.

Chang Chung-yuan. *Original Teachings of Ch'an Buddhism*. New York: Random House, 1969.

Cleary, Thomas, trans. and intro. *The Book of Serenity*. New York: Lindisfarne Press, 1990.

————, trans. and intro. *The Flower Ornament Scripture: A Translation of the Avatamsaka Sutra*. 3 vols. Boston: Shambhala Publications, 1985–1987.

————, trans. and intro. *Timeless Spring: A Soto Zen Anthology*. Tokyo: Weatherhill, 1980.

Cleary, Thomas, and J. C. Cleary, trans. *The Blue Cliff Record*. Boston: Shambhala Publications, 1992.

Cook, Francis Dojun. *How to Raise an Ox: Zen Practice as Taught in Zen Master Dogen's Shobogenzo*. Los Angeles: Center Publications, 1978.

Cook, Francis H. *Sounds of Valley Streams: Enlightenment in Dōgen's Zen*. Albany: State University of New York Press, 1989.

Donner, Neal Arvid. "The Great Calming and Contemplation of Chih-i," chap. 1: "The Synopsis." Ph.D. diss., University of British Columbia, n.d.

Dumoulin, Heinrich, S. J. *The Development of Chinese Zen*. Translated by Ruth Fuller Sasaki. New York: First Zen Institute of America, 1953.

Eido Mui Shitsu. "White Cloud." *ZCLA Journal* 3, nos. 3, 4 (1973): 50–53.

Eitō Sokuō, ed. Shōbōgenzō. 3 vols. Tokyo: Iwanami Shoten, 1939–43.

Fields, Rick. "Buddhist America," Unpublished manuscript (later reedited as *How the Swans Came to the Lake*).

————. *How the Swans Came to the Lake: A Narrative History of Buddhism in America*. Boulder: Shambhala Publications, 1992.

Fujiyoshi Jikai. *Zenkan Sakushin*, Zen no Goroku Series, No. 19. Tokyo: Chikuma Shobō, 1970.

Hakeda, Yoshito S., trans. *The Awakening of Faith*. New York: Columbia University Press, 1967.

Hurvitz, Leon, trans. *Scripture of the Lotus Blossom of the Fine Dharma*. Translated from the Chinese of Kumārajīva. New York: Columbia University Press, 1976.

Inagaki Hisao. *A Dictionary of Japanese Buddhist Terms*. 5th ed. Kyoto: Nagata Bunshodō, 1992.

————. *A Glossary of Zen Terms*. Kyoto: Nagata Bunshodō, 1991.

————. *The Three Pure Land Sutras: A Study and Translation.* Kyoto: Nagata Bushodō, 1994.

Kapleau, Philip, ed. and trans. *The Three Pillars of Zen.* 25th anniversary ed. New York: Doubleday, 1989.

Katō Shūkō, ed. *Shōbōgenzō Yōgo Sakuin.* 2 vols. Tokyo: Risōsha, 1962–63.

Ketelaar, James Edward. *Of Heretics and Martyrs in Meiji Japan.* Princeton: Princeton University Press, 1993.

Kim, Hee-jin. *Dōgen Kigen: Mystical Realist.* Tucson: University of Arizona Press, 1975.

Kitagawa, Joseph M. *Religion in Japanese History.* New York: Columbia University Press, 1966.

Kodera, Takashi James. *Dogen's Formative Years in China: An Historical Study and Annotated Translation of the Hōkyō-ki.* Boulder: Prajna Press, 1980.

Lu K'uan Yü (Charles Luk). *Ch'an and Zen Teaching.* 3 vols. York Beach, Maine: Samuel Weiser, 1993.

Maezumi, Hakuyu Taizan, *The Way of Everyday Life.* Los Angeles: Center Publications, 1978.

Maezumi, Hakuyu Taizan, and Bernard Tetsugen Glassman. *The Hazy Moon of Enlightenment.* Los Angeles: Center Publications, 1978.

Miura Isshū, and Ruth Fuller Sasaki. *Zen Dust: The History of the Koan and Koan Study in Rinzai (Lin-chi) Zen.* New York: Harcourt, Brace and World, 1966.

Mizuno Kōgen, et al. *Shin Butten Kaidai Jiten.* Tokyo: Shunjūsha, 1966.

Nakamura Hajime. *Bukkyōgo Daijiten.* Tokyo: Tokyo Shoseki, 1981.

Nakamura Sōichi. *Shōbōgenzō Yōgo Jiten.* Tokyo: Seishin Shobō, 1975.

Ōkubo Dōshu. *Dōgen zenji den no kenkyū.* 2nd ed. Tokyo: Chikuma Shobō, 1971.

————. *Dōgen Zenji Zenshū*. 3 vols. Kyoto: Rinsen Shoten, 1988.

Okumura Shōhaku, trans. and intro. *Shōbōgenzō-zuimonki: Sayings of Eihei Dōgen Zenji Recorded by Koun Ejō*. Kyoto: Kyoto Sōtō Zen Center, 1987.

Okamura Shōhaku, and Taigen Dan Leighton, trans and intro. *Bendōwa: Talk on Wholehearted Practice of the Way*. Kyoto: Kyoto Sōtō Zen Center, 1993.

Powell, William F., trans. and intro. *The Record of Tung-shan*. Honolulu: University of Hawaii Press, 1986.

Price, A. F., and Wong Mou-lam. *The Diamond Sutra and the Sutra of Hui-neng*. Boulder: Shambhala Publications, 1969.

Robinson, Richard. *Early Madhyamika in India and China*. Delhi: Motilal Banarsidass, 1976.

Senzaki Nyogen; Soen Nakagawa; and Eido Shimano. *Namu Dai Bosa: A Transmission of Zen Buddhism to America*. Edited with an introduction by Louis Nordstrom. New York: Theatre Arts Books, 1976.

Shibayama Zenkei. *A Flower Does Not Talk*. Rutland, Vt.: Tuttle, 1970.

————. *Zen Comments on the Mumonkan*. San Francisco: Harper & Row, 1974.

Suzuki, D. T. *Essays in Zen Buddhism*. 3 vols. London: Rider, 1970.

————. *Manual of Zen Buddhism*. New York: Grove Press, 1960.

————. *The Zen Doctrine of No Mind*. London: Rider, 1969.

Takakusu, Junjirō. *The Essentials of Buddhist Philosophy*. Edited by Wing-tsit Chan and Charles A. Moore. Reprint. 1956. Westport, Conn.: Greenwood Press, 1976.

Takakusu, Junjiro, et al., eds. 85 vols. *Taishō shinshu daizōkyō*. 85 vols. Tokyo: Taishō Issaikyō Kankōkai, 1924–32.

Terada Tōru and Mizuno Yaoko, eds. *Dōgen*. 2 vols. *Nihon shisō taikei* 12, 13. Tokyo: Iwanami Shoten, 1970–72.

Uchiyama Kōshō. *Genjōkōan Ikai*. Tokyo: Hakujusha, 1975.

Uchiyama Kōshō and Dōgen. *Refining Your Life: From the Zen Kitchen to Enlightenment.* Translated by Thomas Wright. New York: Weatherhill, 1983.

Ui Hakuju. *Bukkyō Jiten,* 8th ed. Tokyo: Daitō Shuppansha, 1974.

Waddell, Norman, trans. "Wild Ivy: The Spiritual Autobiography of Hakuin Ekaku," Part Two. *The Eastern Buddhist* 16.1 (1983): pp. 107–139.

Waddell, Norman, and Abe Masao, trans. with intro. "Shōbō-genzō Genjōkōan." *Eastern Buddhist* 5.2 (1972): 129–40.

Yamada Kōun. "The Stature of Yasutani Hakuun Roshi." *Eastern Buddhist,* new series 7.2 (1974): 108–20.

————, trans. with commentary. *Gateless Gate.* Tucson: University of Arizona Press, 1990.

Yampolsky, Philip B., trans. and intro. *The Platform Sutra of the Sixth Patriarch.* New York: Columbia University Press, 1967.

Yasutani Hakuun. "My Childhood." Translated by Taizan Maezumi from *Zen and Life.* Fukuoka: Shukosha, 1969. In *ZCLA Journal* 3, nos. 3, 4 (1973): 32–35.

Yasutani Hakuun. *Shōbōgenzō Sankyū: Genjōkōan,* Tokyo: Shunjūsha, 1967.

Zengaku Daijiten Hensansho. *Zengaku Daijiten.* 3 vols.: Daishukan Shoten, 1978.

Made in the USA
Middletown, DE
08 November 2016